PRAISE FOR HOLY COW!

"If animals could read, they'd love this!"

Doris Day
Founder and President of The Doris Day Animal League
Actress

Holy Cow!

Holy Cow!

DOGGEREL, CATNAPS, SCAPEGOATS,
FOXTROTS, AND HORSE FEATHERS—SPLENDID
ANIMAL WORDS AND PHRASES

★

Boze Hadleigh

Skyhorse Publishing

Skyhorse Publishing books may be purchased in bulk at special discounts for sales promotion, corporate gifts, fund-raising, or educational purposes. Special editions can also be created to specifications. For details, contact the Special Sales Department, Skyhorse Publishing, 307 West 36th Street, 11th Floor, New York, NY 10018 or info@skyhorsepublishing.com.

Skyhorse® and Skyhorse Publishing® are registered trademarks of Skyhorse Publishing, Inc.®, a Delaware corporation.

Visit our website at www.skyhorsepublishing.com.

10 9 8 7 6 5 4 3 2 1

Library of Congress Cataloging-in-Publication Data is available on file.

Cover design by Rain Saukus

Print ISBN: 978-1-63220-557-5

Ebook ISBN: 978-1-63220-952-8

Printed in China

In memory of Rusty—
all cats go to heaven.
In admiration of Doris Day,
In appreciation of Ronnie and Linda, and
In praise of animal activists—
we are their voice....

ACKNOWLEDGMENTS

For invaluable help and support, thanks again to Linda and to Ronnie.

At Skyhorse (beautiful name), thanks to my enthusiastic, savvy editor Alexandra Hess. Also to Marianna Dworak and to Cheryl Lew.

Thanks as well to Judy Benesh, Eddie Espinosa, Earl Holliman, Lorri Jean, Sue Kutosh, Louie Magenheim, Jeff Olson, Mary Stark, Sarah Wheeler, Betty White, and late friends and animal activists Bea Arthur and Chad Oberhausen, and the late Dr. Betty Berzon.

TABLE OF CONTENTS

INTRODUCTION

Have you ever called someone a rat or a mouse, a sheep or a leech, a barracuda, a pig, or just plain chicken? How about bats or batty, catty, a social butterfly, a lounge lizard, a snake, or slothful? Ever seen anyone get mad as a wet hen?

How seldom we think about how often we attribute negative human traits to innocent beasts, itself a term of contempt. By the way, the correct expression is "Music hath charms to soothe the savage breast," not the savage beast. It's from a Congreve play, *The Mourning Bride*, of 1697. Time to get it right.

Here, in five chapters spanning the animal kingdom—dogs, cats, horses, other mammals, non-mammals—you'll find the origin stories and the definitions of hundreds (at least!) of animal-related words, phrases, and expressions.

A very few are of unknown origin, like charley horse for a cramp, taking a gander (a look) at something, a ratcatcher suit, sick as a lizard, or dingbat. Why bats, or for that matter, nuts, are associated with madness is unknown. A possible explanation is the seeming craziness of bats sleeping upside-down.

Some expressions make little sense at first. Like to cow someone, when she's such a gentle animal. But the phrase reflects her considerable size and may have been coined at a time when cows were less docile. Some words get slotted into an expression simply because they fit. Like none of your beeswax for none of your business. Nothing to do with bees. But did you know that in the 18th century people sometimes filled in facial pockmarks with beeswax, which is still an ingredient in many cosmetics?

What, though, is so cute about a bug in a rug?

In ancient times a new, unusual animal was often compared, usually unrealistically, with another, more familiar one. For instance, porpoise in Latin was a *porco marino*, a sea pig! And so we have a sea lion. Also a sea elephant, which is an elephant seal. Did you know a monkfish is an angel shark? (How on earth, or in sea, does angel relate to shark?)

As a child, when I first heard of a towel horse I thought it was like a teddy bear but made of terrycloth (who or what was terry? "Unknown origin"). Towel horse typifies many animal terms that represent what an animal does or is "for." In this case, one puts something on a horse—usually a person. So you can have a sawhorse or a towel horse or a clotheshorse, which was originally something to put clothes on. But language, like animals, evolves, so now a clotheshorse is, well, a fashionista.

Some animal names are imprecise. Did you know almost any invertebrate that's much longer than it is wide is called a worm? Worms, it turns out, are the majority of all animal life on earth—or under earth. And "little worms" in Italian is *vermicelli*, today thin pasta, but centuries ago, the generic name for all non-stuffed pasta until the word *maccheroni*, later *macaroni*, replaced it.

Rarely, a person is compared to an animal in a positive or neutral way—a lamb, a dove, or a sea dog, who is an old or experienced sailor. Speaking of dogs, sometimes through Latin translation a word ends up quite different, e.g., kennel is from Old French *chenil* via Latin *canis*, dog. French words easily become mispronounced in English, as with *chamois*, originally made of goat, sheep, or deerskin for cleaning or polishing and originally the name of a southern European mountain goat-antelope. Since it's invariably pronounced shammy in English, chamois is now often spelled that way—or called shammy leather.

In French, a *canard* is a duck. In English, a canard is also an unfounded rumor or story, from the Old French *caner*, meaning to quack, which signified a hoax (which has nothing to do with calling a lousy doctor a quack, as you'll see).

Why is an unattractive or old woman called a crow? It boils down to sexism, and is related to crone, an ugly old woman, from Middle English via Middle Dutch, meaning an old ewe or carcass, related to the word carrion. As for eating crow, gentle reader, read on.

To conclude on an avian note, in classical fables the crow was a thief, stealing more attractive feathers of others to beautify himself (male birds are prettier, like the peacock). In Renaissance literature the crow or upstart crow—many bookstores are named after the latter—is a plagiarist. In his day, Shakespeare was called an upstart crow, implying that the mysterious man from Stratford, whom nothing connected with the writing of plays and who was possibly illiterate, may have stolen or more likely fronted the plays written by educated courtiers who feared Elizabeth I's potentially fatal censure. Which reminds us that there's sometimes more savagery in the human breast than in a beast or animal.

One way or another, people have always been drawn to animals, and as this book shows, they permeate our language. Fortunately, in a modern age freer of superstition and prejudice—and ironically less dependent on animals—we better appreciate our non-human cohabitants and now realize it's their planet too.

Boze Hadleigh
Beverly Hills
May 15, 2015

DOGS

Hot Dog

A hot dog in the 1890s was often human, usually in college. The phrase could be complimentary, as with most phrases including "hot," but typically denoted a showoff. A 1995 issue of *Comments on Etymology* gave a sample of 1897 collegiate slang: "Brown's a hot dog, isn't he?" "Yes, he has so many pants."

Dialect Notes in 1900 defined a hot dog as "one very proficient in certain things," which by the 1960s evolved into the verb "to hot dog," referring to the expertise of sometimes show-offy surfers, skiers and skateboarders. A hot-dog board was a short surfboard, more easily ridden than longer, heavier ones. Hot dogs enjoyed performing stunts, generally while skiing or surfing.

Soon, baseball players were labeling their more flamboyant, attention-seeking teammates hot dogs. The 1979 book *Bronx Zoo*, about the New York Yankees, called

Tito Fuente "One of the most renowned hot dogs in baseball history." In 2005 the *New York Times* described snowboarders "hot-dogging" down a mountain. Hip-hop slang also uses dog, misspelled dawg.

Hot Dogs

When non-English speakers first hear the culinary term hot dog, they're usually appalled until the name is explained. The "invention" of hot dogs is hotly debated, with myriad claims for credit, nearly all by Germans or German Americans. In 1987, Frankfurt, Germany, celebrated the frankfurter's 500th birthday, its origin shrouded in myth and public relations.

Back in the 1600s a butcher named Johann Georghehner from Coburg, Bavaria, created a dachshund sausage named after the small, long-bodied German canine. In England the comestible became known as a little dog, while dachshunds were eventually nicknamed sausage dogs.

Johann took his sausage to Frankfurt, where it became a hit and was soon renamed a frankfurter—like natives of that city. A wiener is a native of Vienna (Wien in German). Whereas frankfurters or franks were made of pork, wieners or weenies were traditionally a pork-beef mixture. By the 1850s, sausage meat was often nicknamed dog's paste, owing to sometimes valid rumors of unethical manufacturers including ground-up dog meat in their product.

In 1871 immigrant Charles Feltman opened a sausage stand in Coney Island, which became renowned for them. In 1882 another kraut—sorry, German, but they do eat lots of sauerkraut—named Christian von der Ahe bought the St. Louis Brown Stockings and commenced the close association between baseball and hot dogs by lowering the ticket price to 25 cents, thereby assuring himself of crowds who would pay considerably more for his frankfurters and beer. (Humphrey Bogart later declared, "A hot dog at the ballgame beats roast beef at the Ritz.")

In the late 19th century "hot dog" emerged as a nickname for both the sausage sandwich and the human show-off. Anti-German sentiment during World War I caused "frankfurter" to go out of favor and boosted "hot dog." Until World War II, hot dogs were often known as red hots because of another Bavarian, Anton Feuchtwanger, who in the late 1800s sold hot sausages to Americans who borrowed white gloves to handle the sizzling item. The gloves kept getting stolen until Anton's wife suggested replacing them with a specially shaped bun …

Another German immigrant, Oscar Mayer, started branding his popular meats in 1904 and built the first Wienermobile in 1936 (in 1963 the company introduced the advertising jingle that begins, "Oh, I wish I were an Oscar Mayer wiener").

The leading US retailer of hot dogs is 7-Eleven (currently Japanese-owned), and the biggest hot dog ever was created by the All-Japan Bread Association in 2006. The wiener measured 196.85 feet (60 meters) long, tucked into a 197.8 foot (60.3 meter) bun. Hot diggity-dog! That expression—a yet more enthusiastic version of the approving "hot dog!"—dates from the early 1900s.

Funny that hamburgers, even more prevalent than hot dogs, didn't evolve into slang words or phrases. Hamburgers, not made of ham, are of course named after the city and residents of Hamburg, Germany.

Human Dogs

Most expressions referring to humans in a canine way are unflattering to dogs and reveal the expressions' age. For instance, a dull dog is a person with little or boring conversation.

A lucky dog is someone with undeserved good luck, reflecting the attitude that dogs deserved little more than a bone. A desperate dog is deemed beneath contempt. Similarly, a dirty dog was either an evil character or, humorously, a sly fellow (a sly dog?) who achieves his ends using devious means.

Originally, a sly dog was a man discreet about his pleasures or one who kept his vices or weaknesses to himself. Now it's often more literal—somebody deceitful or cunning ("sly" derives from an Old Norse word meaning cunning). When it comes to successfully hunting for food, say, most animals are capable of feinting, but cunning canines?

When someone is termed a clever dog, it's not usually a compliment that they're smart, but that one way or another they get what they want.

Somebody leading a dog's life was ill-treated or had a miserable life. If an actual dog's life was such, it was (or is) typically due to a human. What else would make a dog dog-tired?

The dogs of war originally referred, as in Shakespeare's *Julius Caesar* (published 1623), to the resultant horrors of war, later on to the politicians, generals, mercenaries, and arms merchants who profit from war.

James Garner, who played a dog robber in the 1964 movie *The Americanization of Emily*, set in England during WWII (Emily was played by Julie Andrews), defined a dog robber as "the personal assistant of a general or admiral whose job it is to keep his man well-clothed, well-fed, and well-loved during the battle."

If somebody dies like a dog, they die without honor or dignity or in shameful circumstances.

A watchdog was an official or authority supposedly guarding the public interest. The positive intent switched to a primarily negative one once authority and its motives became questioned more often.

An underdog was the assumed loser in a two-dog fight. In the more compassionate societies of today—those which are—the negative has primarily changed to positive, as most everyone roots for the underdog.

Two men and a dog used to mean very few people. Every man and his dog meant everybody.

You Dog…

Sadly, humanity's best friend has often been considered anything but in numerous times and places. In today's "Third World," dogs are often no more than tolerated—and visibly underfed. Where humans go hungry, one can't expect much compassion for canines. Then there's religious dogma (which noun has nothing to do with dogs). Islam's founder Mohammed deemed cats clean yet dogs unclean. To call somebody a dog remains a serious insult in many countries.

Until about 150 years ago, the only good dog was a useful dog. The ancient Egyptians bred dogs to have chondrodysplastic, or dwarfed, legs that compelled them to trail game at a pace with which humans on foot could keep up. The Egyptians used other dogs, bred for speed, power, and tenacity that could overtake gazelles and kill them minus human assistance.

In the United States as recently as the 1960s, a song ("So Long, Dearie") lyric from *Hello, Dolly!* deprecates a man as "you dog." Now seldom heard, anti-canine epithets are mostly confined to novels and old movies. They reflect a time when the "lowly" dog was scapegoated with specifically human traits, as in "you lying dog" (or hound, more widespread in Britain).

In Australia and New Zealand, "to turn dog on" means to inform on someone or turn traitor.

A dog in the manger harkens back to the fable about the dog who lay in a manger to keep the horse and ox from eating the hay he himself didn't want. It still refers to a selfishly contrary person who prevents others from having what he or she doesn't want or need.

"It shouldn't happen to a dog" implies it shouldn't even happen to someone as low as a dog. "Every dog has his day" indicates that even a dog occasionally receives a bit of good luck or fortune and is used to counsel patience—good luck comes eventually.

In Germany there's a double insult: *Schweinhund* (pig-dog), which the *Collins German-English English-German Dictionary* understatedly defines as a dirty fellow or cad.

"Dog eat dog" doesn't refer to the desperate hunger that can lead to cannibalism in any species but, rather, to the sort of cutthroat competition, typically to do with business or politics, unknown to any species except homo sapiens.

Mutt, now often used affectionately toward any dog, is short for muttonhead, which derives from sheep. In the 1800s muttonhead referred to an incompetent or stupid person; mutt was applied to mongrel dogs on the theory that mixed breeds (animal or human) were less intelligent than purebreds.

Cur

Like humans, dogs can be aggressive. Cur refers to an aggressive dog, often a mongrel, but came to be slang (per the *Concise Oxford English Dictionary*) for a despicable man.

Mongrel, which denoted a dog of indefinable—therefore more than likely mixed—breed, came to mean, in a very humanly mean-spirited way, a person of mixed origin. What was sometimes seen as undesirable in a dog was often viewed as awful or unacceptable in a person.

Many people would agree that dogs' least desirable trait is excessive barking. Why don't dogs get sore throats or laryngitis after extended barking? A canine's vocal range is narrower than a human's and its less delicate larynx or voice box isn't as prone to stress and temporary damage. Arf-arf!

Bitch

Patriarchy has traditionally regarded women as psychologically closer to animals than men are, even though characterizing a human as a beast invariably applies to a grown male, typically in a violently sexual context. The ancient Greeks believed only females could become hysterical and fall into hysteria, both related to "hysterectomy," all from their word for womb: *hustera* or *hystera*.

A bitch is a female dog (or wolf or fox or otter). Female animals' purported misbehavior was often projected onto women. For a long time, "bitch" was considered semi-obscene; the 1939 film *The Women* finds Joan Crawford insulting a group of well-to-do ladies by declaring there's a word for them that's not usually heard outside a kennel. Today the word is routinely and widely heard.

The dictionary also defines "bitch" as a woman who is spiteful or disliked. A double standard of dislike still tends to cling to women, especially if very successful or very attractive or not attractive.

In recent times, bitch took on a non-human, non-canine situational meaning, as in the gloomy aphorism "Life is a bitch, then you die."

In black English, bitch means woman. Oddly, bitching (often misspelled bitchen) came to mean, as an adjective, excellent, and as an adverb, extremely.

Son of a bitch, an entrenched insult, is unthinkingly sexist, for who does it really insult? The *mother* of whomever one is trying to insult. (It's worse in Spanish, where the phrase translates as son of a whore.) Contrast this with son of a gun, which is admiring of both father and son.

A final insult, to both canines and women, is the use of dog to mean an ugly woman. (No epithet for an ugly man.) Before animals were thought of as pets, many or most people seemed unable to discern beauty in beings other than human. But as Leonardo Da Vinci, generally considered history's greatest genius, said of the cat, "'tis a thing of beauty and a living work of art." (Woof?! Steady, Fido.)

Seeing a Man about a Dog

The Victorian era was known for prudery and hypocrisy, traits which often combine to produce euphemisms. One such was to go "see a man about a dog." It signified, even in unmixed company, one's unexplained intention to depart present company to engage in a, ahem, delicate activity. Often a visit to a prostitute. The expression later came to mean an excuse to depart for any reason. In the United States during Prohibition (1920–1933) it became a euphemism for going to purchase illegal liquor.

In the Old West men often bought liquor at low-class watering holes known as dog-holes or doggeries. The latter may have resulted from crossing dog with groggery. Grog was a nickname for spirits (originally rum) mixed with water. In time, individuals leaving for an unacknowledged drink or snort dropped the dog and simply said they had to go see a man.

By the late 20th century "seeing a man about a dog" became widely used by women too—though they still went to see a mythical man—and had changed implication, for prostitution, liquor, betting, and such were replaced by the call of nature. As in *The Third Deadly Sin*, a 1981 novel by Lawrence Sanders: "'Make yourself at home,' Fred said. 'I gotta see a man about a dog.' He went into the bathroom, closed the door."

More Human Dogs

A lapdog is an overly pampered person or child or somebody completely under another's influence. Conversely, a top dog is someone who makes himself dominant or master. When these expressions began, before electric saw mills, logs were positioned over specially dug pits. Two men used a long saw; one stood in the pit and got covered in sawdust—he usually protected his throat with a scarf—while the other sawyer remained at ground level and guided the saw while it cut. The paired but unequal jobs were called top dog and under dog (vs. the underdog that lost a dog fight).

(Another kind of sawyer—besides Tom—is a big insect whose larvae bore tunnels inside wood.)

A dogsbody is someone, usually starting up the professional ladder, given boring or menial tasks.

In Australia and New Zealand a dogman is he who operates a crane while sitting on a crane's load.

A gay dog used to mean someone pursuing an idle lifestyle while displaying the symbols of (usually inherited) wealth. Or it was a young man with an active romantic life. Now it would refer to a homosexual or bisexual canine.

Talk about projection: a human wearing a hangdog expression or having a hangdog air is said to look dejected, guilty or shamefaced.

Love me, love my dog—the person saying this may or may not have a dog but wants to be liked as an individual, flaws and all, or requires an intimate to also like their friends and perhaps pets.

To dress up like a dog's dinner, used more often in Britain, is to wear godawful clothes and usually refers to a female.

A hound dog is an odd thing to call one's girlfriend, even if she's "cryin' all the time," as in one of Elvis Presley's early hits. The lyric adds that she's no friend of his because she "ain't never caught a rabbit." The lyric was originally penned for a woman to sing about her disappointing man.

A hot dog (see prior entry) was sometimes said by his fellow collegiates—back when very few women went to college—to "put on the dog," or dress conspicuously. Today the phrase signifies trying to impress, usually without notable apparel. Putting on the dog might refer to, say, a costly dinner prepared for special guests—at which hot dogs (the culinary kind) would never be served (though caviar, or fish eggs, quite possibly).

Nouveau riche Americans in Europe who socialized with local moneybags were said to put on the dog because some of their wives spent small fortunes acquiring fancy little dogs to put on their laps for show.

Sic 'im!

Sic 'im!—the command to a canine—means Get him! To sic, originally meaning to find, is a corruption of the German word *such* (pronounced zooh—heavy h—from the verb *suchen*, to seek or look for). It's used by trainers of guardian, tracking, and police dogs, and orders the animal to locate a hidden perpetrator or victim. Trainee dogs are only supposed to attack if the sought human tries to run away or hit the dog. But thanks to the dramatic misinformation typical of most movies and TV, "sic" in the popular imagination means a command to attack. Which usually it is not.

If you've wondered why wet dogs wait to shake the water off until they've gotten close to their masters, the reason is endearing rather than annoying. A domestic canine's desire to return to its master's side after a wetting experience is temporarily stronger than its wish to shake itself dry.

A Dog...

It takes "A dog's age," or very long time, to suffer through "a dog's life." Why dogs became associated with taking a long time is a mystery, especially as their lifespans are much shorter than humans'. As for a dog's life being dreary or downtrodden, hopefully it isn't to the dog concerned. Unless the poor animal has to "work like a dog," which would be thanks to a human. ("Dog-tired," invariably applied to people, also harkens back to when dogs had forced careers.)

"A dog's breakfast" (or dinner) is British slang for a mess. This seems more apt for a pig than a canine (which, after all, buries its bone), but was coined in a pre-canned-dog-food era when the meal of a dog or cat ("a cat's breakfast" means the same) was often leftover scraps tossed on the floor—by a human who didn't put them in a dish.

"A dog-and-pony show" is North American slang for a fancy or overdone presentation or event. Like, say, a political convention or some TV sports productions.

A dog collar is an irreverent nickname for a clerical collar but was also slang for the stiff high collars once required of Yale University students—all were male—on formal occasions.

A dog clutch mechanically pairs two shafts—one slotted, one with teeth—so they can initiate motion. A dogtrot is an easy gentle trot and a dog cart is a two-wheeled cart for driving in which originally included a box beneath the seat for the hunter's dogs (charming, eh?).

Ungraciously, a dog end is the last and least desirable part of something. In Britain it also means a cigarette end or butt. A dog-leg is a sharp bend or a golf hole where the fairway bends, the former reminiscent of the angle of a male dog's leg lifted to pee.

A dogger is either a big rounded concretion in sedimentary rock or a "two-masted bluff-bowed Dutch fishing boat" (what else?).

A doghouse is a pooch's abode or a raised standing area at the rear end of a yacht's coachroof—well, of course. To be in the doghouse is to be in disgrace or disfavor.

A dogwatch on a ship runs from only four to six or six to eight p.m. (however, some are late-night, when on land supposedly only a dog would be awake). A possible origin of the term is the claim that the Dog Star is the first to be visible in the evening sky, while one wag has suggested that the abbreviated watch is cur-tailed.

A dogshore is either of two timber blocks placed on each side of a ship to prevent it sliding. A firedog, also known as an andiron, is one of a decorative pair of metal supports for wood burning in a fireplace.

A Dogrib isn't canine fast-food, but a Native American from northwestern Canada or Alaska. Dogrib, or "dog's flank," is also a name for their Athabaskan language and stems from the legend that their common ancestor was a dog.

Hair and Bones

"The hair of the dog" is a laughably curative phrase that goes back to when English doctors prescribed "the hair of the dog that bit you." That is, rubbing the hair of the dog that bit you into the wound it made (doctoring often used to be a sideline for barbers). The theory was that like cures like. Over the centuries, hair of the dog became associated with alcohol, the idea—or excuse—being that a drink or two the morning after would diminish the hangover. Wonder what AA has to say about that.

"A bone to pick" originated in the 1500s when the sight of a dog chewing on a bone till it was picked clean put somebody in mind of two humans with a symbolic bone to pick—talking (or hashing) out a problem until it was solved or picked clean. Likewise and in the same century, a bone of contention over which two dogs fought came to represent two humans (with a mutual beef) arguing.

Doggone Phrases

Some ailurophobes have expostulated the dog's superiority over the cat by pointing out that dog is God spelled backwards. In English, anyway. But did you know that the ejaculation Doggone! (or Doggone it!)—usually uttered with an exclamation mark—is attributable to a 19th-century euphemism, dog on it, that avoided the then-taboo God damn it?

To lie doggo parallels to play possum in its meaning of lying quietly and still so as to avoid detection. Unlike its cousin, this phrase's origin is unknown.

Dogged, as in dogged pursuit, obviously references the tenacity of most dogs once they've gotten hold of a scent (or a frisbee, etc.).

To "go to the dogs" means to deteriorate markedly or go downhill. It may be related to Britain's the dogs, which means greyhound racing. For, if a man often went to the dogs, a gambling addiction was likely and penury possible.

Doggerel, originally humorous verse composed in irregular rhythm, later (because of the prefix dog-) acquired the contemptuous connotation of poorly written verse or words. Similarly, dog Latin—unlike the jocular pig Latin—denotes a debased form of Latin. Thumb through a book carelessly or often enough and its corners become dog-eared, doggone it.

Dogtrot is an obsolete American name for a *porte cochere* (literally, coach door or gate), a covered entrance or porch where cars stop to disgorge passengers.

Dog days are the hottest part of the year—when a dog gets hot under the collar—reckoned in ancient times from the simultaneous rising of the sun and Sirius, the brightest star in the sky. Sirius is the Dog Star, which appears to follow on the heels of Orion the hunter.

Soldiers wear identifying dog tags, dandies may sport a dogstooth pattern, flashier dressers might prefer the larger houndstooth pattern, and dogs'-teeth—small pointy moldings—adorn (since the 12th century) the apses, arches, arcades or archivolts of some buildings.

A dog's-tooth, or noticeable notch, is also found on the edge of an airplane wing or tailplane, for instance, on the F-4 Phantom and F-15 Eagle. It was first used in the Wright brothers' Flyer IV.

Dogs' Feet

"My dogs are killing me!" is a remark heard in myriad old movies, usually from a woman (no lady) relievedly removing her shoes. A British variation dating back at least a few centuries was "My dogs are barking!" Linguist Mario Pei theorized that dogs became associated with feet because they have twice as many as humans—thus, twice the potential for sore feet—and that although a more logical remark would be "My paws are killing me!" paws are generally considered closer to hands than feet, since dogs use their front paws for digging.

Question: Do a dog's feet ever get tired?

A perhaps apocryphal story has a German or Hungarian movie director advising an uninspired Hollywood star that an actor's emotions should emerge "during the dog's feet." The star was bewildered and annoyed by the director's repeated phrase until an assistant explained that the director meant "during the pawses."

Doggy...

The dog is a standard, used by humans more often than any animal but the horse in comparisons with other beings and things—as this book makes doggedly clear. Sometimes the canine connection was only in the eye of a few beholders but the name or phrase stuck anyway.

Not much style to doggy-style, but Noel Coward managed a classy answer when a friend's small child asked why one dog was standing so close behind another dog on the village green. Sir Noel declared that the first dog had taken ill and the second dog was very kindly pushing it toward the nearest hospital.

The doggy-paddle, now better known as the dog-paddle, is a basic swimming stroke resembling that of a dog.

Doggy bag is a euphemism pertaining to the uneaten restaurant food one takes away to eat later. It could as easily have been a kitty bag, but the g's in "doggy" complement the g in bag better.

Doggy Biz

The names of real businesses catering (mostly) to our best friend:

All Dogs Go to Heaven Crematorium—in Brighton, England

Citizen Canine—a dog kennel in Oakland, California

Collie Flowers & Hearts—a doggy gift-shop-on-wheels in Toronto, Canada

Doggie Style—a dog-grooming business in North Highlands, California

Doggy 'Do—a dog hairstyling salon in Sydney, Australia

Ms. Gooch's Pooch Obedience Academy—in Dunedin, New Zealand

Murphy's Paw—a doggy gift store in Pleasanton, California

Paws & Refresh—a nail-trimming and shampooing spa in Cincinnati, Ohio

Tail o' the Pup—a hot dog stand in Los Angeles, California

Wagga Wagga Canine Beauty Salon—in Wagga Wagga, Australia

Canine Critters

The bulldog, with its powerful protruding lower jaw, was originally bred and trained to bite into a bull and hang on until the bull died. In rodeos and the like, to bulldog—or bulldogging—is a human wrestling a steer to the ground by holding his horns and twisting his neck.

A bulldog ant is a sizeable Australian ant with big jaws and a potent sting. But a bulldog bond is a sterling bond issued on the British market by a foreign borrower, while a bulldog clip is a patented spring metal device with two flat sides that close to hold papers together.

The smallish cocker spaniel of the silky coat and soulful eyes was bred to flush game birds such as woodcock. Likewise, the name of the amiable terrier belies its origin as a tenacious breed used to turn out various animals, including foxes (so, fox terriers), from their earths. The word derives from Latin *terra*, earth.

A dog whelk is a predatory marine mollusk seen on shore or found in shallow waters, while a spur-dog isn't an animal, but a mechanical device for gripping.

If a catfish is a fish with whiskers, what's a dogfish? It's a small shark with a long tail. Bow-wouch.

Everyone's heard of bats in the belfry—up where the bells are kept, in a bell tower or steeple, symbolizing a batty person's brain. An alternative, seldom heard now, was bulldogs in the belfry, used by Ray Bradbury in his 1981 story "Colonel Stonesteel's Genuine Home-Made Truly Egyptian Mummy."

Garden Dogs

Dogwood is so named because its hard wood was used to make "dogs" or skewers.

A dogberry is a fruit of poor eating quality from a dogwood or other shrub or tree.

Dogbane (compare to wolfsbane) is a plant reputedly poisonous to dogs; bane was an old name for poison.

Dogstail is fodder grass with spiky flower heads.

Dog's mercury is a plant with hairy stems.

A dog violet is a scentless wild violet, but a dog's-tooth violet is a member of the lily family with backward-pointing curved petals (*Erythronium dens-canis*).

Hound's tongue is a tall plant with tongue-shaped leaves and—get this—a mousy smell.

Little Dogie

In most westerns, it's clear when the cowboy says or sings, "Get along, little dogie," that he's addressing a calf. A dogie may be an abandoned or motherless calf (sometimes because she's been recently slaughtered), but not usually. When fans wrote to Republic Studios in the 1940s inquiring about dogies, one publicist replied that the name was owed to compassionate cowboys replacing the calf's mother with a dog for a companion, sometimes tethering the two together.

That explanation has been discredited. Rather, some cowboys called a calf a dogie after the Spanish *dogal*, a halter or noose that keeps a calf away from its mother while she's being milked. Dozens of anglicized cowboy terms came from Spanish, such as vamoose from *vamos*, let's go, and buckaroo, which evolved—or devolved—from *vaquero* (*vaca* means cow).

Can It

The idea of putting a stop to something or someone overlaps the concept of making them disappear. Can it!—meaning stop it—is over a century old. Helen Green's 1908 *The Maison de Shine* includes the order: "You can that stuff!"

The expression evolved from the cruel practice of tying a can to a dog's tail, then starting to chase it—whereupon the frightened animal, hearing the scary, noisy attachment, runs all the faster, disappearing from the area and probably never returning. This led to "tying a can to somebody"— a human—to get rid of him. Another 1908 novel, *The Call of the South* by Robert Lee Durham, depicts an angry political rally in which the mob tries to drown out a dissenter with shouts of "Shoot the dog!" and "Tie a can to his tail!"

The tail part of the expression eventually became obsolete, leaving just the can. Over the decades and via umpteen movies and TV programs, *Can it!* became synonymous with Shut up. In time that usage also diminished. Today, "getting canned" means being fired—in other words, a stop to one's employment.

(The Animal Legal Defense Fund [aldf.org] is trying to establish a national animal-abuser registry "to give animal shelters and law enforcement a way to keep track of animal abusers in their area and keep animals out of the hands of these violent criminals." The ALDF asks, "Is community service enough for torturing and killing an innocent dog?")

Mascots

By the early 20th century dogs had earned an almost entirely benign image—who knew from pit bulls then?—and were coming into wide use to advertise products. (Mascot comes from the French word for sorcerer.) One of the earliest and longest-lasting product mascots was Nipper of RCA fame, who listens to "his master's voice." Its inspiration was a real fox terrier named Nipper who supposedly, at his master's funeral, was mesmerized by a recording of the dead man's voice and stared into the phonograph's horn, his head slightly cocked in puzzlement.

In time, RCA advertised their Color Trak television and video equipment using Nipper's son Chipper. (Notice that nearly all canine—and other animal—mascots are devised as male.)

Mack Trucks, with their snub-nosed hoods and ability to perform well under duress, were nicknamed bulldogs in World War I. In 1922 the company adopted a bulldog as their advertising mascot and in the '30s, a bulldog became the hood ornament on Mack trucks.

Greyhound Bus began in 1914, when many US roads were unpaved. The company's bus (singular) was painted gray because any other color would look dirty after hours on the road. When somebody remarked that the bus resembled a greyhound streaking across the landscape, the company's founder chose the slogan "Ride the Greyhound" and adopted the speedy animal as its symbol.

Bristol Laboratories employed a coughing dog to pitch Naldecon-CX cough syrup, to get rid of "barking coughs." The American Brake Shoe Company used Stopper, a long-haired terrier shown skidding to a stop in its ads. Then there was the Ken-L-Ration Dog. It makes sense having a dog, albeit not a real one, advertise dog food, even if it pops its eyes and lip-smacks its tongue anticipating just one specific brand of dog food.

Dalmations were integral to pre-motorized fire depart-ments. Running ahead of horse-drawn firefighters, they would clear the way for them to reach fires as quickly as possible. Honoring Dalmations' past bravery and service, many fire departments still use them as mascots.

Hush Puppies

In the Southern US, catfish has traditionally been served with fried cornmeal biscuits. Hush puppies came from the latter's batter (deep-fried). In the period of poverty following the Civil War, mothers often served up bits of fried corn batter to quiet the hungry cries of children and dogs, often adding, "Hush, child," or "Hush, puppy."

The cornmeal morsels were also tossed to noisy dogs by hunters to quiet them down—"Hush, puppy!"

The South also had a salamander called a hush puppy, sometimes called a water dog or water puppy. Only the very poor were reduced to eating these amphibians; reportedly, some whispered among themselves, "Hush, don't tell anyone."

Puppy...

The word puppy may derive from the French *poupee*, doll or toy, from a Latin word meaning doll or girl that also evolved into poppet and is related to puppet. Once upon a time, a puppy show was a puppet show. Because of the sexist assignment of dogs to males and cats to females, in Britain until recently a puppy was a young man, often arrogant or one who conceitedly corrects his elders. In the United States, puppy may be used in a specifically ironic way, as in "He is one sick puppy."

To be or act puppyish is usually to be playful and applies to boys as well as girls, unlike kittenish. "The evening's still a pup" means the evening is young. Puppy love (and the less frequent calf love) is associated with adolescents and immature first loves or crushes. Puppy fat usually disappears at or soon after adolescence.

To "sell someone a pup" is to gyp them by misrepresenting something.

A pup tent is an American term for a small—thus, pup—tent for one or two people that's triangular and has no side walls.

Why does a mother dog circle several times before settling down to feed her blind and deaf newborns? A prime reason is to spread her scent and let the pups know where and how far away she is. Dogs' habit of circling before lying down is partly territorial and harkens back to life in the wild and tamping down a sleeping area among leaves and tall grass.

Barking Up the Wrong Tree

This phrase harkens back to 19th-century North America, when raccoon-hunting was common. Hunters would scour the woods at night, stalking the nocturnal creatures whose name comes from the Algonquin *aroughcun*. Dogs were used to pick up the scent of the frightened prey, who would scurry up the nearest tree.

Barking dogs standing with their paws against a tree trunk gave away the presence of a raccoon above. A hunter would typically climb the tree to grab the prize (fortunately, the poor creatures have sharp claws), but if for some reason the raccoon wasn't there—perhaps having escaped to the branch of a neighboring tree—the hunter would decide or announce that his dog had been barking up the wrong tree.

Davy Crockett was credited with originating the regional colloquialism, but more likely he popularized it. A variation appeared in *An Account of Colonel Crockett's Tour to the North and Down East*: "Some people are going to try to hunt for themselves ... (but) seem to be barking up the wrong sapling."

The canine employed was often a coonhound, a specifically bred black-and-tan American dog. In *Sketches and Eccentricities of Col. David Crockett of West Tennessee*, Crockett described it as "the meanest thing on earth, an old coon dog barking up a tree." (Coon was also a derogatory nickname for a black man.)

A Shaggy Dog Story

This phrase meaning a story that's hard to believe derives from a real one retailed at fashionable London dinner parties during the 19th century. It concerned a Park Lane resident who lost his beloved shaggy dog while walking it through Hyde Park. He prominently advertised his loss in *The Times*.

A sympathetic American in New York City read about the ad and determined to seek out a shaggy dog matching the description and present it to the bereaved gentleman the next time he visited London.

When the Yank rang the doorbell of the Englishman's mansion, he encountered a snooty butler who glanced at the dog and pronounced, "Not as shaggy as *that*, sir." Members of London's upper crust enjoyed the story but weren't sure they entirely believed it.

(*The Shaggy D.A.* (1976), not the first Disney movie about a man in dog's clothing, was also hard to believe.)

Hound...

Hounds were bred for hunting, particularly via their sharp sense of smell. Before the concept of pets, dogs were expected to earn their keep—usually by helping humans hunt other animals—just as domestic cats were primarily mousers, to help keep the grain supply intact. A deerhound, for instance, is a big, rough-haired breed that resembles a greyhound. In time, hound became a reference to dogs in general. (Dog in German is *Hund.*)

Because hounds were so dogged (!) in their quest for prey, to hound became synonymous with persistent pursuit, or what might now be called harassment. That word derives from the French *harasser*—to set, sic, or sick (a dialect variation of seek) a dog on another creature, by way of the Germanic *hare*, a yell egging a dog on to attack.

A publicity hound persistently seeks the limelight. It was often applied to Paris Hilton with or without her chihuahua in hand or handbag.

Hound is also used in the names of assorted dogfish, for example the nurse hound, a large spotted fish found in the northeast Atlantic. The name is from nusse, a Middle English word of unknown origin, and has nothing to do with doctors' underrated assistants. Nurse, an Australian shark also known as the grey nurse, is the ironic moniker for a razor-teethed predator found in shallow inshore waters.

Chow

A chow is a thickly furred Chinese dog with a bluish-black tongue whose tail curls over its back. In Mandarin Chinese chow means to fry or cook, as in chow mein, from *chao mian*, fried flour or noodles. In Cantonese Chinese chow means food—chow dogs were originally bred for food and emphatically named chow chow.

In 18th-century America chow became occasional slang for food ("let's chow down," etc.). A chowhound is an enthusiastic eater, as one dictionary kindly puts it, and has nothing to do with chowderhead, US slang for an unintelligent person.

More Mascots

In 1961 the Wolverine Shoe & Tanning Company introduced a line of soft-soled shoes called Hush Puppies, the name
indicating both quietness and the suppleness of puppies. To
advertise them they chose a placid bassett hound. (Bassett
comes from the diminutive of French *bas*, meaning low, for
the dog, besides its droopy ears and long body, has short legs.
A wolverine, its name derived from wolf, is a sturdy short-
legged carnivore found in the forests and tundra of North
America and Eurasia.)

Another bassett hound, famous on the East Coast, was Axel-
rod, the mascot for Flying A Gasoline. The pooch wore a wor-
ried expression that tied in with the company slogan, "When it
comes to your car…Ooooh, do we worry!" (Ooooh, brother.)

In 1963 Quaker Oats hired animator Jay Ward, creator of
Rocky (the flying squirrel) and Bullwinkle (the big moose), to
advertise its sugary new cereal, Cap'n Crunch. The befuddled
captain's first mate was named Seadog and was a sea dog. The
pair, with the aid of a crew of children, spent their time averting
the attempts of dastardly pirate Jean LaFoote to steal their cereal.

The controversial Spuds MacKenzie debuted in 1983,
highlighting and high-life-ing Bud Light beer. He was often
seen partying poolside with young beauties collectively
named the Spudettes. Spuds ignited sales of Bud Light but
became too popular with teenagers and was later drafted to
warn the public about the dangers of drinking and driving.

A fleeting scandal erupted when it was discovered that the dog who played him was a female. By then, most people knew that Lassie had often been enacted by a canine laddie.

The Poodle Cut

The story goes that in the 1950s some French female aristocrat was giving a party and had her hairdresser cut and style her poodle's hair into a fluffy bob with bangs (fringe in England). The pooch was the hit of the party, inspiring the hostess to have her hair cut and styled the same way. The boyish 'do spread through France and Italy—Gina Lollobrigida was one of the first stars to wear it—then arrived in the States and was taken up by women of all ages, including a style-conscious but mature Joan Crawford. The most famous example of the poodle cut was Audrey Hepburn, specifically in the 1953 film *Roman Holiday*, in which her character, a princess, has her humdrum long hair shorn by an Italian coiffeur into the perky, fashionable new 'do.

Poodle...

The phrase *as pampered, happy* or *as comfy as a poodle on a pillow* may or may not have been conceived by ex-actress Jacqueline Susann, whose book *Every Night, Josephine*, about her beloved black poodle, sold poorly. It was then she decided to throw all the stops out and write a novel called *The Valley of the Dolls*.

Poodles have long been considered foppish, partly due to their mincing gait. The styles in which their curly fur is sometimes clipped often look risible but reflect more on the owner than the choice-less dog. In fact, many consider the poodle the most intelligent breed, perhaps a reason it seldom becomes aggressive. It is, however, sensitive and can become jealous of children in the human family.

Over the last century or so, especially outside France and Germany, the poodle has become associated with women, and poodlefaker is a now-obsolete British term for a man who cultivates women's company—with no real interest in their pooches (the word "pooch," though said to have originated in the 1920s, is of unknown origin).

The expression "I'm nobody's poodle" isn't a canine lament, but a person's (usually a man's) assertion that he has a mind of his own or is not easily led by others. Woof!

The French poodle is internationally famous, yet the breed most likely began in Germany, then was taken to France. Its name is from German *Pudelhund*, from *puddeln*, to splash in water (related to English puddle), for the poodle is a water dog.

A mix lately gaining popularity is a schnoodle, a cross between a schnauzer and a poodle. (The former derives from Schnauze, German for snout.) Guess what hybrid a piggle is? A pit bull and a beagle.

Bark

Country singer Mel Tillis once asked, "How can a dog's bark be worse than his bite? His bark don't hurt you none." For humans, however, it's a valid expression for somebody who may seem gruff—like, say, Mary Richards's boss Lou Grant—but who's really a pussycat.

Tillis also explained that as a boy he was a big fan of Lassie and wanted a collie, until relatives said that if he got one, people might be apt to say, "Here comes Mel and collie."

The phrase "All the dogs are barking" signifies that a piece of news is being widely disseminated.

The phrase "Why keep a dog and bark oneself?" means, for example, Why hire a cleaning lady and then do the dusting oneself?

Negative Expressions

Unlike a cat, the more gregarious dog will voluntarily follow its master's steps. But in the past, when society chose to view even domesticated animals negatively rather than appreciatively, this touching fact yielded the plaintive expression to dog one's steps. The 1966 *Dictionary of American Idioms* gave this dated example: "All the time he was in Havana, Castro's police were dogging his steps."

"Give a dog a bad name and hang him" indicated how hard it is to alter a bad reputation. *Longman's Dictionary of*

English Idioms explains that "If a dog is said to bite or be bad-tempered, it might as well be killed because no one will trust it any more."

The happily obsolete expression "Any stick will serve to beat a dog" indicates that one can always find fault with someone if one wants to, any excuse will do. A kinder expression, to help a lame dog over a stile, meant to aid a struggling person (a stile was steps set into a wall or fence to let people climb over).

To throw something to the dogs is to sacrifice something.

"As sick as a dog" comes from the false assumption that a dog will eat anything thrown its way.

"The tail wagging the dog" is when a minor aspect of something has a disproportionate or major influence.

"To let sleeping dogs lie" is akin to not waking a sleeping dragon, to refrain from provocation, to leave well enough alone and avoid trouble.

"You can't teach an old dog new tricks" isn't true and seems to shift the effects of human aging onto canines.

More positively, to "Call off the dogs" is to abandon an audit or investigation when it's leading nowhere—as when huntsmen called off their dogs when they'd gotten hold of a false scent.

"Does a dog have fleas?" means "Does a bear do it in the woods?" (The opposite of "Does a snake do push-ups?")

CATS

Swing a Cat

"Not enough room to swing a cat" means too small a space. Although the term's visual image now seems bizarre, even humorous, it was once all too literal. As we know, some cultures elevated the cat while others denigrated it. Ancient Egypt literally adored felines, but Christianity traditionally deprecated cats, one reason being their reputation as "familiars" of witches (usually women practicing non-Church-approved remedies and rituals). Thus, hundreds of thousands of cats were hung or burned at the stake along with their female owners over the centuries.

There are two explanations for this phrase. A cat-o'-nine-tails was a rope whip with nine knotted cords in it, used to flog British sailors. The punishment (discontinued in 1875) left scars on a man's back resembling cat scratches and took place on-deck because inside a cabin there was "not enough room to swing a cat-o'-nine-tails" (originally three cords).

One of many inhumane "sports" in medieval Europe was swinging cats by their tails to serve as moving overhead targets for archers at fairs, festivals, and holiday events. If a given event was particularly crowded, it was sometimes reported there wasn't enough room to "swing a cat."

Other "sports" included cat tossing and cat burning. Not wishing to possibly undermine its own agenda, the Church didn't interfere with such sadism. This was true of both major Christian sects; a 1554 engraving depicts a cat, dressed as a priest, that was hung at an anti-Catholic demonstration in London.

A Cat-in-Hell's Chance

Like the also obsolete a dog's chance or a "Chinaman's" chance, this phrase means no chance at all. But it's incomplete. Originally it was "no more chance than a cat in hell without claws." Cats have far less chance anywhere without their claws. Interesting that theirs are retractable, while dogs' claws aren't. Unfortunately, those who dislike cats view this positive trait as a negative. Napoleon, a known ailurophobe (he once screamed when a cat entered his tent in Egypt), called retractile claws a proof of perfidy.

As most cat lovers know, declawing a cat is no kindness. It's less like clipping fingernails than amputating fingers up to the first knuckle (visit www.pawproject.org).

More Than One Way to Skin a Cat

Cat lovers, relax. This phrase stating there's more than one way to perform a task or achieve a goal has nothing to do with Muffy, Bitsy, or Thomasina. It's about catfish, a fish easily caught but not easily skinned. The several ways to do it include dropping one into boiling water before unpeeling it.

Why was it called a "catfish"? Because somebody with wretched eyesight thought its "whiskers"—barbels, from the Latin *barba*, or beard—made the homely scavenger resemble a cat (by contrast, Leonardo Da Vinci pronounced the cat a living work of art). As to why the phrase-ending was shortened from catfish to cat, one can only speculate that some ailurophobe was being dogmatic.

Traditionalist male authors often treated cats and supposed feline (read: feminine) traits more harshly than they did dogs. An example is a sentence from Part III of Nietzsche's *Thus Spoke Zarathustra* (1883), his most famous philosophical work: "For I would sooner have even noise and thunder and weather curses than this suspicious, dubious cat-like stillness, and also among human beings I hate the most all pussyfooters and half-and-halfers and doubting, hesitating, drifting clouds." (What a sourpuss!)

Cat...

A catsuit is a skin-hugging one-piece item of womenswear that includes pants. It's usually meant to be provocative, more so if made of leather, vinyl, or rubber—remember Michelle Pfeiffer as the Catwoman? Or, earlier, Julie Newmar? Either would have stopped traffic (by the way, America's bumper-to-bumper traffic is Britain's nose-to-tail traffic).

A catcall is a whistle or shout expressing disapproval. The term dates back to the 1600s. (Contrast it with a wolf whistle.)

The defining quality of a catwalk is its narrowness, whether a platform for models to parade on or a vertiginous walkway or skinny bridge in an industrial installation or elsewhere—cats of course being known for their agility, straight-ahead gait, and lack of fear of heights (except when stuck in a tree).

A catfight is between two women. Note that a dogfight isn't between two men, though it may be between military planes. Cat is a long-standing nickname for a prostitute and, via sexist association, sometimes for a female, hence a catfight.

A cat nap is fairly brief and usually taken sitting up. It's a refresher.

A catlick is British slang for a casual wash, the opposite of what a real cat would do.

Cat ice is the dangerous thin ice beneath which the water has receded.

Cat's cradle is a classic children's game that uses a length of string held between each hand's fingers to create assorted patterns.

Of course many words beginning with the prefix cat- have nil to do with felines, including catsup, catalepsy, catamite, cataclysm, catacomb and catalog(ue).

Cathouse

Since at least 1401, Englishmen were warned of the risks— including often fatal venereal diseases—of chasing "cat's tail," vulgar slang for female genitalia (remember, vulgar originally meant common). Prostitutes were nicknamed cats because urban she-cats attracted and copulated with so many tom-cats. Hence the term cathouse, where female prostitutes live and/or do business.

Ironic that venereal, the adjective for Venus, goddess of love and beauty—the Roman version of the Greeks' Aphrodite—is today (unlike in Shakespeare's time) used almost exclusively in that one negative context.

Cat People

Cats don't get fat unless people make them so. They're often finicky eaters, to the extent that cat food manufacturers use humans to test cat food because cats refuse to. Fat cats are rich or overpaid people in positions of influence, such as heads of corporations, often including non-profits. They're often resented and sometimes corrupt.

A cat burglar usually robs houses and gets in by shimmying up a drain pipe and entering through an upper-storey window (this probably happens mostly in movies).

Copycat, used particularly by children and competitors, is apparently alliterative in origin, another example of a cat being viewed more negatively than a dog.

Somebody with the morals of an alley cat is typically someone who will sleep with anyone else (think Blanche on *The Golden Girls*).

Someone who is catty is spiteful, often while feigning interest or sincerity. Almost always used about a woman, as in "She told her hostess, 'My dear, I love that dress. I never tire of seeing it.'"

A hellcat is defined as a spiteful, violent woman. Likewise, grimalkin is an archaic word for a cat but also signifies a spiteful old woman. (Malkin was a familiar form of the name Matilda.)

The British expression to "Lead a cat and dog life" refers to a married couple who argue often and loudly, the implication being they don't get along, like the stereotypical cat and dog, who in reality are nowise enemies.

A cat's paw is somebody who is used by another or others. Similar to a stalking horse but worse, in that the equine equivalent often involves politics (see the chapter Horses), but a cat's paw may be fooled or forced into undertaking an unpleasant or dangerous task.

Jazz musicians have long labeled someone they approve of as a cool cat. Pre-hippie beatniks bestowed the word hep on whatever was, well, hip. It's no longer hip to call someone a hepcat, but Audrey Hepburn's 1956 movie-musical debut *Funny Face* proclaimed, "Hepburn Goes Hep!!"

Curiosity and the Cat

Why did curiosity kill the cat and not, say, the dog? Aren't dogs much more interested in what humans do than cats? Alliteration played a part. According to psychologist Betty Berzon, "Curiosity is stereotypically affiliated with women, so this is a cautionary proverb warning women to mind their own business. If curiosity began with a different letter, it's possible a cat might not be the victim."

The full expression was: Curiosity killed the cat but satisfaction brought it back. The second half is rarely invoked, for it mitigates the warning in the first half. What does the second half mean? Two interpretations prevail: the dead cat was satisfied with what it found out, and her death was worth it, since she still had eight lives to go. Or, the satisfaction of keeping out of trouble—and minding one's "own business"—prevented kitty from going too far and brought her back from the brink of death.

Ever been curious why cats' and dogs' eyes, more than humans', sometimes appear red in photographs? It's because the light from a camera's flash penetrates directly to the lens of the eye, then is reflected off the retina—the eyeball's back surface—then bounces back to the camera. The red one sees in the photo is blood. Cats and dogs have bigger, more open pupils than people, which lets the flash enter their retinas more easily.

To Grin Like a Cheshire Cat

The most famous example of the expression "to grin like a Cheshire cat" occurs in Lewis Carroll's *Alice's Adventures in Wonderland* (1865), made vivid by John Tenniel's wonderful artwork. However, *The Classical Dictionary of the Vulgar Tongue* (1788) already included the expression, defining it as someone "who shows his teeth and gums in laughing." Did Carroll posit a widely grinning cat or, more specifically, one with a sarcastic streak who taunted Alice?

Betty MacDonald, who wrote adult and children's fiction, including the Mrs. Piggle-Wiggle books, felt, "Carroll served up the anomaly of a smiling cat, since animals can't smile— well, perhaps some primates—and emphasized it with a leer of a smile. By the time the cat disappears from the story, all that remains of it is its smile … the one thing it never had. That's Carroll's perverse sense of humor."

MacDonald believed the expression derived from cheeses made in Cheshire, England, molded to resemble a grinning cat. As slices were cut away, it was possible to end up with the head, then just the smile.

Others believe the grin was inspired by a cat carved on St. Wilfrid's Church tower in Grappenhall, a village near the

Cheshire town where Carroll, *né* Charles Lutwidge Dodgson, was born. Others claim the descent is via a cat or lion "with a strange smile" (sometimes described as a feline Mona Lisa) emblazoned on the coat of arms of the Grosvenors, an influential Cheshire family.

Yet others say the progenitor of the phrase was one of Richard III's forest rangers, an enthusiastic swordsman from Cheshire who also terrified poachers with his wide, sadistic smile. His last name was Caterling, ergo a "grin like a Cheshire Caterling."

In any case, the expression conjures up the one about the cat who swallowed the canary, another feline whose self-satisfied smirk implies but doesn't reveal.

Catgut

Most people know it's not made of any part of a cat—and never was. In *Much Ado About Nothing* (1600) Shakespeare wrote, "Is it not strange that sheep's guts should hale souls out of men's bodies?" (Hale then meant haul.) Musical instruments' strings and surgical sutures are made of dried, twisted sheep, horse, or ass intestines. How cats entered the musical fray is unknown. An educated guess is that people compared the sound of a badly played violin to … caterwauling.

Speaking of musical instruments, a fortunately only theoretical one was a cat organ or cat piano (*Katzenklavier* in German). Nonetheless, various Europeans—especially Frenchmen and Germans—wrote about it in the 1700s and before. The concept was several cats arranged in a row according to their voices' natural tone, their tails stretched out beneath a keyboard so each would cry out in mutually harmonizing pain when a key was struck. Sick minds.

The Cat's Pajamas, Whiskers, and Meow

Flappers were the female "young moderns" of the 1920s, also known as jazz babies or cats (the latter often implied sexual laxity). Pajamas or pyjamas (British spelling) were a fairly new women's fashion item. In 1922 the *New York Times* described an unknown woman (a publicity hog?) who landed in the newspaper by strolling Fifth Avenue dressed in yellow silk pajamas, in tandem with four pet cats similarly dressed!

The flapper or cat and her pj's combined to form what progressives of both genders (American women got the vote in 1922) considered the latest "in" thing. During that deliberately daring decade—sandwiched between the horrors and disappointment of the Great War (WWI) and the economic and psychological trauma of the Great Depression—youth and the media made popular catchphrases of the "cat's paja-mas," "the cat's whiskers," "the cat's meow," and "the bee's knees" (young women's knees were sometimes on display and they didn't get arrested for it).

In the United States, these phrases meant tip-top, A-1, the best to be had. Cat's pajamas could also refer—as in "She thinks she's the cat's pajamas"—to someone's conceit. Besides being an excellent person or thing, cat's whiskers were the fine adjustable wires in a crystal radio receiver. As television later swept the country during the 1950s, radio swept the USA in the Roaring '20s.

(Cat hairs are more electrostatic than dog hairs, hence kitty cling. But another reason cat hairs stick to clothes more than those of other pets is their microscopically small but very rough barbs.)

Catnip

Catnip is an American term for catmint, a member of the mint family formerly used to make a popular tea, plus juice, infusions, tincture, and poultices. People also smoked and drank it. The US word evolved in the 18th century—nip from *nep* from *Nepeta cataria*, Latin for catmint. The herb's leaves have short soft hairs, its white flowers are spotted with purple, and the pungent scent attracts most but not all cats. How catnip internally affects felines is unknown, but it affects females and males in the same way, as well as some big cats like tigers and lions. Lynx and bobcats crave catnip. Alas, it's sold commercially to lure and trap them.

The stages of an affected cat's response to catnip are: sniffing, tasting with head shaking, chin and cheek rubbing, head-over rolling, and bodily rubbing. The experience lasts less than 15 minutes but may include vocalizing—possibly a reaction to hallucinations. (Catnip is not a feline aphrodisiac.)

Most experts agree that younger cats react more strongly to catnip than older ones and that the first experience is the strongest.

Cat Plants

Cattail or cat's tail is a reed mace—a tall water plant with a velvety dark brown cylindrical flower head that feels like a cat tail—or other plant with thin long parts resembling cats' tails.

Cat's foot is a small creeping plant with white flowers and soft white hairs on the leaves and stem. Though it sounds like a fuzzy sweater, it's a member of the daisy family.

Pussy willow is a willow with soft, fluffy catkins— hanging, wind-pollinated flowering spikes, so named from Old Dutch *katteken*, meaning kitten.

Cats, like dogs, are carnivores and, unlike humans, can't thrive on a vegetarian diet. If you've wondered why cats often eat sitting up while dogs eat standing up, it has to do with dogs being pack animals—a pet dog's human family is its adopted pack. In the wild, members often must compete for food scraps, easier to do standing up. Cats, being more solitary hunters—excepting lions—have the mental luxury of eating more slowly and in a more comfortable crouch.

Puss, Pussy

The word puss evolved in the 16th century from German or Dutch, a name for a cat, its diminutive being pussy (formerly also spelled pussie). Puss is also American, Scottish, and Irish slang for someone's face, as in "What a cute puss you have," from Irish *pus*, meaning lips or mouth. Plus it's a coquettish young female, though a glamour-puss isn't typically limited by age.

A puss moth is a big, furry, gray-white moth with darker markings.

Why *pussy* became vulgar slang for female genitals incurs a myriad of theories, some very fanciful, like the old-time aristocratic female habit of sitting with a cat or pussy in one's lap. Most likely it's a textural comparison.

To pussyfoot is a negatively connoting verb for behaving overcautiously or non-committally or to move stealthily or sneakily. More positively, it's aiming soft physical or verbal blows not intended to hurt an opponent—referencing a cat's soft paws.

Pussy-whipped, a recent derivation, is sexist slang for a female-dominated man (no term for a male-dominated female).

A pussycat bow is a big, soft, floppy bow at the neck of a woman's blouse.

Ding-dong-dell, pussy's in the well … notice how the majority of kiddie-lit feline references are negative—for example, the cat in the original *Pinocchio* represents hypocrisy—or take pleasure in a cat's dilemma. A notable exception is the tomcat hero Puss in Boots.

Cat Animals

Why are male cats toms? "The Life and Adventures of a Cat" was an anonymous English story published in 1760 that became extremely popular. Its male protagonist was called Tom, and soon so was every other male cat.

Catkin is a kitten or small cat. The –kin suffix, now practically obsolete, was a common English diminutive, as in the old-fashioned Daddykins—or lambkin.

Catamount is from cat of the mountain (when rarely used it's sometimes confused with the non-feline catamite). A catamount is a puma or any medium- or large-sized wild cat. A puma is a mountain lion, also known in North America as a cougar.

More recently, a cougar is a woman who—like Cher, say—pairs with younger men. Psychologist Dr. Betty Berzon offers, "It's better than 'dirty old woman,' which would parallel a 'dirty old man' who prefers younger women. It's too bad 'cougar' has a slightly predatory feel to it. On the other hand, there is a somewhat admiring connotation to this new meaning."

"Cat among the pigeons," incidentally also the title of an Agatha Christie novel, means stirring something up by introducing a controversial topic, as in mentioning the ex-husband of your hostess at her dinner party. The original phrase was to throw a cat among the pigeons, thereby creating shock, fear or anger.

A civet is a slender nocturnal cat from Asia and Africa with a barred *and* spotted coat whose scent glands contain a powerful musky perfume much in demand in the fragrance industry (see Musk in Chapter 4). A smaller version of the civet, the linsang, is native to Southeast Asia.

Angora refers to a cat, rabbit or goat or to the fabric made from the latter two's hair; it's the old name for Ankara, now the capital of Turkey.

Cat Clowder

A gaggle is a group of geese (also a bunch of disorderly people). Why "gaggle"? One dictionary says it's imitative of the sound a goose makes. Uh-huh. We say a bevy of quail—no one can claim "bevy" is imitative of quail—but a bevy is also any sizeable number of things or people, beauties or not. Herd, often heard with cows, isn't specific to them; it means a large number of animals, particularly hoofed mammals that live or are kept together (it's derogatory when referring to a big group or class of people).

There's an entire vocabulary of names for groups of specific animals, most going back centuries and many having no particular logical derivation. A few animals have various terms, such as kennel, litter or pack for dogs and stable, team or harras for horses. The majority of such terms are little-known. Some examples:

- a clowder or a glaring of cats
- a gang of elks
- a bale of turtles
- a labor of moles
- a sleuth of bears
- a crash of rhinos
- and a leap of leopards (not lizards)

- a kine of cows
- a float of crocodiles
- a dray of squirrels
- an army of frogs
- a shrewdness of apes
- a drift of hogs

Non-Cats

A North American term for skunk is polecat, though it's a member of the weasel family. Again, less common animals were often named or nicknamed after a primary animal they more and often less resembled. The pole-part of the term is from an old French word for chicken, a favorite meal for skunks (modern French for chicken is *poulet*, related to English pullet, a young hen).

The cute, sometimes standing-up meerkat has become much more familiar thanks to TV programs like *Meerkat Manor*. It's a small southern African mongoose whose name is Afrikaans—the language of South Africa's Dutch colonists—for seacat. The mongoose, famous for killing snakes in India and elsewhere, wasn't named after a goose. Its name in India's Marathi language is *mangus*.

A bearcat is a Southeast Asian bearlike climbing mammal, including the red panda (pandas aren't bears), apparently so named because they climb trees agilely.

A catbird is a North American songbird with catlike mewing calls.

The prominent "whiskers" of the unattractive bottom-feeding catfish act as sensory organs, helping it to navigate and find food (it's dark down there). The reputation of catfish as scavengers prevented many people from consuming them, but today farm-raised catfish are also available.

Copycat is an alliterative misnomer, as any cat owner knows. A dog is much more inclined to copy or try and reproduce a human's action or gesture. Small schoolchildren like to yell "Copycat, copycat!" at fellow offenders. The ongoing allure of alliteration is proven by its frequency in headlines, captions, and sometimes titles.

To Let the Cat Out of the Bag

Nowadays, letting the cat out of the bag means inadvertently revealing something, usually a secret. In medieval times, it meant a shopper ("To market, to market, to buy a fat pig") had been had. Those who could afford one would barter or haggle for a piglet on display. After a deal was struck, while the buyer was distracted, a cat might be substituted for the little pig in the bag—no paper or plastic, of course. Once home, the hornswoggled shopper would let the cat out of the bag. Which probably later led to a fight back at ye olde marketplace.

This leads to the phrase "buying a pig in a poke." Meaning sight unseen. "Poke" is a chiefly Scottish term for a bag or small sack (related to the French "poche," pocket). *Caveat emptor*, for inside the unexamined poke could be any smallish animal—though you'd think any cat in a bag would make its presence audible long before the shopper returned home.

P.S. Despite its beginning with horn—the origin of hornswoggled is unknown.

Mascots

Surprisingly, "unlucky" black cats have been used more often in advertising than other colors. Two examples: Cat's Paw Rubber Heels—"non-slip"—and Eveready Batteries, the latter because of the myth that cats have nine lives.

Tigers go back to 1913 as mascots for gas companies. Humble Gasoline employed one, and in 1959 the Oklahoma Oil Company launched its slogan "Put a tiger in your tank!"

It's been said that in cereal advertising the top dog is Tony the Tiger, who bowed in 1952 on packages of Kellogg's Sugar Frosted Flakes, which he shared with Katy the Kangaroo (can you believe it). In the 1970s cereal companies dropped the word "Sugar." Originally, Tony stood on all fours, later evolving into a bi-ped. He was given a son, Tony Jr., whom he eventually taught the alleged value of Frosted Flakes. Tony Jr., solo, sold Kellogg's Frosted Rice cereal. Tony Sr. also had a wife and daughter who later disappeared, as did the son, replaced by real human children.

Another still-popular big-cat mascot is Chester the Cheetah, who advertises Cheetos cheese puffs.

(Black cats were deemed unlucky because of the association between black and Hades or "hell." In the western world black is the color of death (e.g., the Black Death) and mourning—in East Asia the mourning color is pure white, signifying departure from a corrupt world.)

Raining Cats and Dogs

One of the most famous animal declaratives is "It's raining cats and dogs." There's no one definitive explanation of its origin. However, in English, "dog" and "frog" rhyme, and through the centuries tales were repeated about actual windstorms when frogs were swept up by a strong gale, then dropped out of the sky—raining frogs. Cockney rhyming slang eventually changed "frogs" (wouldn't a rain of frogs be gross?) to the more appealing "cats and dogs" (though a shower of felines and canines would also be rather startling).

Additionally, some cultures believed cats held sway over storms, especially at sea, hence the numerous nautical terms with feline references. The Vikings usually included dogs in myths and illustrations of their god of storms. Thus, many northern Europeans held cats responsible for rain and dogs for gales. (Probably no connection, but the surname of dog-lover Dorothy in the book *The Wonderful Wizard of Oz*— where she wore silver, not ruby, slippers—is Gale.)

"Raining cats and dogs" made its bow, or bow-wow, in literature in 1738 via Jonathan Swift, the Irish author of *Gulliver's Travels*. In *A Complete Collection of Polite and Ingenious Conversation*, he wrote, "I know Sir John will go, though he was sure it would rain cats and dogs."

In his 1653 play *City Wit*, Richard Broome predicted, "It shall rain dogs and polecats." Of course in North America polecat now means a skunk.

Nine Lives

Probably the first culture to believe cats had more than one life was the ancient Egyptian, where cats were deified—the cat goddess was Bast or Bastet—and well treated as pets. On the other hand, being adored had its drawbacks (i.e., sacrifice). A huge percentage of cat mummies found in temple precincts have been of kittens and young cats. Why? So priests wouldn't have to spend as much feeding them as longer-lived cats. (The ritual murders were usually done by snapping their necks.)

Yet pet cats were pampered and esteemed. That, plus their natural caution and ability to survive falls from considerable heights, gave some people the impression that cats lived on and on. The expression that cats had nine lives dates back to at least the 1500s, as so many do. Nine may be the result of the favored Christian number three (Trinity...) multiplied by itself.

Kitten...

A kitten is also the young of other animals, like beavers and rabbits. The word is used in the names of various furry gray and white moths.

To kitten is to give birth to kittens, but in Britain to have kittens is slang, usually about females, for being very nervous or upset or even hysterical. In medieval Europe it was believed that if a pregnant woman experienced pains, "She was bewitched and had kittens clawing at her inside her womb." Desmond Morris in his 1986 *Catwatching* explained that up through the 17th century "an excuse for obtaining an abortion was given in court as 'removing cats in the belly.'"

A kitten heel is a modified high heel usually worn by a girl or very young woman.

"As weak as a kitten" means feeble or very weak (notice it's not as weak as a puppy).

To be kittenish is to act playful or flirtatiously or foolishly younger than one's age. As with most things kitten, it's mostly reserved for females. Kitten used to be a favorite nickname for a younger daughter—as in the TV series *Father Knows Best.*

The reason one doesn't see teacup cats, versus teacup dogs, is that feline genes are far less plastic than those of dogs, which are the most genetically malleable of mammals. It's not only difficult to miniaturize or interbreed cats, there's little demand for it. Housecats are relatively small already—in significant ways they're miniatures of the wild big cats.

P.S. Roughly one out of every 3,000 calico cats is a male.

Kit Cat

Why is there a myriad of Kit Cat Clubs the world over (sometimes spelled Kit Kat, as in the movie *Cabaret*)? Kit is a longtime nickname for both Christopher and Katharine (friends of the American stage star called her Kit Cornell). But the first Kit Cat Club was named after a Christopher Cat, in 1703 in London. A cook by trade, Cat was a Whig, a member of Britain's reformist party (equivalent to US Democrats). He held political meetings in his mutton-pie shop, where the group became known as the Kit Cat Club.

Sir Godfrey Kneller painted the portraits of its fourty-two members (they can be seen in London's National Portrait Gallery). Each painting was 28" by 36", less than half-size, a format now known as kitcat.

The Kit Cat Club lasted two decades, but the prestige of its alliterative name was resurrected in more permissive times when Kit Cat Clubs—sometimes styling themselves "for gentlemen only"—sprouted like mushrooms, often as strip clubs (Tom Cat Clubs would be more appropriate). An innocent carryover of the name still accrues to those delicious Kit Kat candy bars.

Kit and caboodle has no feline origin; kit refers to required items or equipment.

Kitty...

Kitty is an affectionate nickname for a cat. It's also a fund of money for communal use or a money pool in certain card games or the small white ball in bowls at which players aim. The word is said to have originated with a kitbag, a canvas bag containing a soldier's possessions but sometimes used to hold the group's pot, or the sum of their bets. To feed the kitty is of course to add to it and make it grow.

Kitty-corner is the North American term for cater-cornered (sometimes cater-corner), also known as catty-cornered. Cater-cornered was first recorded in 1519, as "the point diagonally across a square or intersection," same definition as today. A square has four corners, and the root of the term isn't feline, it's four in French: *quatre*. Note again the tendency to turn neutral words into more familiar or comforting animal words like kitty. Southern US variations include kittywampus, kiddywampus, cattywampus and, yes, caterwampus.

Since we're that close to "caterpillar," did you know it's from an Old French word meaning hairy cat? Now, *that* took some imagination.

Wildcat...

The wildcat is a small Eurasian and African cat, usually gray with black markings, believed to be the ancestor of the domestic cat. It's also a term for any small wild feline, particularly a bobcat, which is a North American lynx with a spotted and barred coat and a short tail, hence the "bob." When someone is said to be lynx-eyed, they have very sharp eyesight.

A wildcat is a fierce, temperamental person, in sexist parlance typically a female. A wildcat is also an exploratory oil well, as well as the verb for to prospect for oil. The title of Lucille Ball's sole Broadway musical, the 1960 *Wildcat*, combined all three meanings.

A wildcat strike is spontaneous and called without the authorization of union officials.

Wildcat is also an adjective meaning commercially risky or unsound, as in a business scheme.

Comic and Cartoon Cats

There are arguably more comic and cartoon cats than any other animal. They came—now that human characters dominate toons and comic strips—in all shapes, sizes, types, and temperaments. Of course there were cat-and-mouse cats, like Jerry's Tom, and cat-and-bird cats such as Sylvester with the lisp, obsessed with capturing Tweety Bird. There were the anonymous villainous felines who threatened but lost out against Mighty Mouse and other mini heroes. There was the ditzy Krazy Kat, a stereotypically lovelorn female, also Mehitabel, an alley cat who was Cleopatra in a past life but currently loved Archy, a cockroach with the soul of a poet.

No-nonsense, problem-solving Felix the Cat was internationally famous in the early 20th century and influenced Walt Disney early on. Dr. Seuss's Cat in the Hat eventually made it out of the book pages, and the 1960s yielded Snagglepuss, a unique pink and possibly gay mountain lion fond of declaring, "Heavens to Murgatroyd." More recently there are Fritz the Cat, Heathcliff, Garfield, and Hello Kitty, et cetera, et catera.

For a time, there was talk of turning the hit musical *Cats* into a TV cartoon series. The time passed, but *Cats* is not forgotten (though many have tried).

Feline Expressions

Few people exclaim "Holy cow!" any more, but even fewer say "Holy cats!" which used to be a common phrase, deriving of course from the ancient Egyptian veneration of felines. Using "holy" in an expression was long believed to avert bad luck or keep evil spirits at bay.

"To bell the cat" is to personally risk danger for the common good and comes from the classic tale of the group of mice who met and decided that it would be an excellent idea to put a warning bell on their feline enemy for their mutual safety. Alas, no one mouse was courageous enough to try and bell the cat.

"In the dark all cats are gray" is obvious and could apply to any animal or thing but became associated in a derogatorily sexual way with women as discussed by disgruntled men (notice one never hears about gruntled employees ...).

"Has the cat got your tongue?" became widespread in the 19th century and has since been shortened to "cat got your tongue?" Originally, it was a presumption of guilt, usually on the part of an adult—including generations of nannies—toward a child. It also was and remains an admonition to a shy child to speak up. For many centuries Europeans believed cats disliked and punished children, also that a cat would perch near a sleeping baby in its cradle, waiting for a chance to "steal his breath."

To play cat and mouse is self-evident. Note that cartoons featuring a cat and mouse inevitably make the cat a villain; it's not sexism, for the cat is almost always male. Rather, it's the David and Goliath syndrome, favoring the smaller being—or underdog.

When the cat's away, the mice will play. So do kids, when the adults are away.

Like the cat that swallowed the canary means being guilty but looking innocent, even elated.

A cat may look at a king is a rare pro-equality proverb from centuries back, a snub to snobbism.

To see which way the cat jumps is to sit on the fence and make a choice only after the majority of one's political party or the public does—that is, an opportunist.

To "kick the cat" is to take out one's anger on an innocent being.

"Like a cat on a hot tin roof"—"a cat on hot bricks," in Britain—denotes somebody very agitated or awkward. The success of Tennessee Williams's play *Cat On a Hot Tin Roof* and its film version gave an added meaning of surviving in difficult circumstances.

Cub

Cub, from the 16th century, is of unknown origin. It refers to the young of a lion, fox, bear, or other carnivorous animal and to a junior branch of the Scout Association, also to any young or new member of a group, for example, a cub reporter.

Chit is widely used in Britain, typically in "a chit of a girl," for a young woman who's impudent, arrogant, or simply disapproved of. The word, whose original meaning was a shoot or sprout, also referred to cubs, kittens, and whelps, a whelp being a puppy, a cub or, derogatorily, a boy or young man.

Dandelion

For reasons unknown to us—maybe they were being pretentious—in the 1500s the English stopped calling what we know as a dandelion a lion's tooth and took up the French name, *dent de lion*, meaning lion's tooth. The spelling and pronunciation mutated with time. Though the flower doesn't at all resemble a lion's tooth, its deeply indented leaves do. (Indent comes from Latin *in* meaning in and *dent* meaning tooth.)

One is reminded of two Brits: Harry says to Alf, "What's the matter, you act like you don't like me anymore." Alf says, "It's not that. It's just that you've become so pretentious lately." Says Harry, "Pretentious! *Moi?*"

Lion...

Europe considered the lion the king of the jungle because the larger tiger was found elsewhere—in Asia—and because of the male lion's impressive mane. So, via the concept that might makes right, the lion's share is bigger than anyone else's. It also derives from Aesop's fable in which a lion and three other animals kill a stag for dinner and divide it into four parts. But the lion, greedy and a bully, insists that as "ruler" he deserves another portion, and then more because of his strength and courage. The final portion he allows the cowed trio to share—if they dare, he warns.

A literary lion is a famous author, heretofore male, while to lionize somebody is to treat them as a VIP.

A lion-hunter is a hostess or host who seeks celebrity guests to impress their friends and other guests.

Lion-hearted means courageous—it should be borne (free...) in mind that most kills made by lions are via the lioness.

A lion's den is an uncomfortable or dangerous place.

A lion tamarin is a small Brazilian monkey with golden or golden and black fur, its cuteness if anything emphasized by its erect lionlike mane.

Lion-colored is an apt adjective when it describes something both majestic and lion-colored, like the sandstone cliffs behind the mortuary temple (Deir el Bahri) of the female pharaoh Hatshepsut near Egypt's Valley of the Kings.

Famous leonine expressions include: to beard the lion in his den—to visit a VIP at their headquarters—to put one's head in the lion's mouth—to foolishly expose oneself to great danger—and to throw someone to the lions—to abandon somebody to a harsh fate.

The British lion is the symbol of Great Britain. Ergo to twist the lion's tail is to provoke or humiliate Great Britain.

Lions and Tamers and Chair

Ever wonder why or if lions are afraid of kitchen chairs? They're not, but any substantial object may be used to control or puzzle a big cat. It was famed lion tamer Clyde Beatty, who trained lions from 1920 till the late 1960s—when he died in a car accident—who introduced the chair. Keeping a lion at bay involves not letting it think it can hurt you, which is why most injured lion tamers complete their act. Running or showing fear turns a human into potential prey. Conversely, approaching a lion, with or without a chair, confuses a lion, for no prey approaches a lion.

The whip that most lion tamers also use provides a noisy distraction.

An alleged life-saving tip if one encounters a lion in the wild (or one escaped from a zoo) is to stay still—do not run away from it. If it begins to crouch, thus commencing hunting mode and a fatal leap, actually run toward the lion and yell. If you dare—oh, my!

Sphinx

The best known sphinx is the giant one carved out of rock near the pyramids at Giza in Egypt, representing the pharaoh Chepren, whose head it bears. Traditionally, a sphinx (sphinges, the plural, is considered archaic) has the body of a lion and the head of a woman, as did the prototype in Greek mythology. She also had wings and killed anyone who couldn't answer the riddle she put to them. The Sphinx's mother was Echidna, who was half woman and half serpent and lived in a cave and ate men.

An echidna is a porcupine anteater—a rare egg-laying mammal—native to Australia and New Guinea (the spiny sea urchin, for instance, belongs to the phylum of Echinoderms). Its name comes from Greek *ekhidna*, viper.

A sphinx is also a mysterious person. Movie star Greta Garbo, who refused to grant interviews, was publicized as the Swedish sphinx.

Sphinx is also a North American term for the hawkmoth, a big, fast-flying moth with a thick body and narrow forewings that feeds on nectar while it hovers. It's a member of the Sphingidae family.

A sphynx is a bizarre-looking hairless cat breed that originated in North America.

Spinnakers, big three-cornered sails set forward of the mainsail of a racing yacht when running before the wind, are named after Sphinx, the 19th-century yacht that was the first to use such a sail.

Tiger Critters

The Tasmanian tiger, also known as a Tasmanian wolf, is a thylacine, a doglike carnivore with a striped rear end. The name derives from Greek *thulakos*, pouch, for the thylacine is or was a marsupial—tragically, it is now probably extinct.

A tiger snake is a highly venomous Australian snake distinguished by brown and yellow bands.

Tiger sharks are more than usually aggressive, live in warm seas, and wear dark vertical stripes.

A tiger prawn, also known as tiger shrimp, is of course a larger shrimp and has dark bands. It lives in the Pacific and Indian oceans.

A tiger worm is a brandling, a red earthworm with brighter stripes used as bait by anglers and in compost.

Various striped butterflies have tiger in their names, for example, plain tiger and scarlet tiger.

A tiger moth is thickset with boldly streaked and spotted wings and a hairy caterpillar known as a woolly bear.

A tiger beetle has striped or spotted wing cases, is predatory and runs fast.

East Asian Tigers

Tiger Balm, a mentholated ointment out of Singapore, is exported worldwide but is especially popular in East Asia. Created in Burma in 1870, its non-English name is Gentle

Tiger, as it's said to combine gentle external pain relief, among other remedies, with the potency of a tiger (one of the Chinese inventor's two sons was named Tiger). After the family successfully transferred to Hong Kong, in the 1930s they built the delightful Tiger Balm Gardens there and in Singapore to show appreciation for the public's endorsement of their product. Sadly, the Hong Kong sculpture garden was razed to make room for an upscale housing development.

(The Japanese good-guy in the fifth James Bond film, *You Only Live Twice*, was called Tiger Tanaka.)

A tiger economy is one of the dynamic economies of various smaller East Asian nations (smaller by comparison with China and Japan), such as South Korea, Taiwan, and Singapore.

A paper tiger is a fake, an adversary of much bluster but little threat. The phrase was repeatedly used by Chinese leader Mao Zedong during the Vietnam war, in reference to the United States and its allies.

Tiger lilies are tall orange Asian lilies spotted (not striped) with black or purple.

Tiger...

A tiger, typically used for a male, is somebody dynamic, virile or both. Tigers are thus often used as icons or mascots for sports teams or products promoting energy, endurance or health (see Tony the Tiger, ironically pitching sugared corn flakes).

A toothless tiger is an authority given inadequate powers or resources to perform its task.

To have a tiger by the tail is to find oneself fighting a bigger adversary or battle than one had thought (bitten off more than one can chew!).

To ride a tiger is to find that what or who you thought you were controlling is controlling you.

A cliché phrase in many romance novels is that a husband should be faithful as a dog but jealous as a tiger.

Tiger's eye is a yellowish-brown semi-precious quartz with a shimmering band of luster.

Tiger Tim was a popular British comic strip in the early 20th century.

Tiger butter is a "striped" (swirled) fudge-like candy usually including milk chocolate, white chocolate, and peanut butter. In the Indian story of Little Sambo, four competing tigers grab each other by the tail, racing around a palm tree faster and faster until all that's left is a pool of butter, or *ghi*, as it's called in India.

A tiger nut is the edible small dried tuber of a type of sedge (a grasslike plant). Doesn't sound very tasty—especially after tiger butter.

A feline-titled movie was *Tora! Tora! Tora!* (1970). Those words were the code name for the Japanese attack on Pearl Harbor—*tora* means tiger.

And a blind tiger, alternatively known as a blind pig, was an illegal bar during the catastrophic US social experiment known as Prohibition.

HORSES

Currying Favor

What would an expression meaning to try and ingratiate oneself have to do with a horse, which has no favors to bestow, or with currying, which is grooming a horse with a currycomb? The answer is that this was no ordinary horse. Favel or Fauvel was the protagonist of an eponymous satirical French romantic poem written in 1310 whose popularity endured for centuries. Favel was a chestnut horse—formerly a centaur, half-man and half-horse—who symbolized cunning and duplicity and could be dangerous. People therefore groomed or curried him to stay on his good side and to benefit from his wiles. With time and the switch from French to English, Favel became Favor, and today one simply curries favor.

Clotheshorse

Also spelled clothes horse. Has nothing to do with how horses look or dress, is related to the more prosaic saw-horse, an American term for a rack supporting wood to be sawn. Likewise, a laundry rack or frame for drying washed clothes derived from the concept of a "horse" being something on which something else is placed, usually a human. The original human clotheshorse was a fashion model, derided (no pun) as a mere frame, typi-cally a skinny one, on which to place or hang a designer's latest creation. Today a clotheshorse is anybody "with a wardrobe to choke Mrs. Astor's pet horse"—a lyric from the 1975 movie musical *Funny Lady*.

Nautically, a sawhorse is a horizontal rail, bar, or rope in a sailing ship's rigging.

The reason a ten-dollar bill is nicknamed a saw-buck is that the latter is a type of sawhorse, which has X-shaped ends. The Roman numeral 10, or X, appeared on ten-dollar bills back when sawbuck was first recorded, in 1850.

Changing Horses in Midstream

Sometimes a leader's use of an expression in a political speech makes it widely known overnight, often in a slightly amended form, as with Winston Churchill's "blood, sweat, and tears." This equine expression about sticking with a course or policy already embarked upon rather than courting disaster through change is often attributed to Abraham Lincoln. However, he made it famous, rather than invented it. During a speech to the National Union League in 1864, the president used it to acknowledge both his nomination for a second term and the fact that many people believed he was mismanaging the Civil War.

Lincoln said the situation brought to mind the story of "an old Dutch farmer who remarked to a companion once that 'it was not best to swap horses when crossing streams.'" Abe felt the League had likewise concluded "that it is not best to swap horses while crossing the river, and have further concluded that I am not so poor a horse that they might not make a botch of it in trying to swap."

The slangy "swap" was eventually replaced with "change," and the warning phrase now is nearly always couched negatively: "Let's not change horses in midstream."

On a more modern, less polite note, the following political graffito was scrawled on many a public-bathroom wall in its day: "Why change Dicks in the middle of a screw/Re-elect Nixon in '72." Had the writers but known about Watergate!

A Mare's Nest...

Before they were called veterinarians, they were horse doctors, as horses were their major patients, also livestock and other farm animals. Treating an ailing cat or dog, or any other pet (say, a parrot), was then considered frivolous, a waste of money and the vet's time. The name comes from the Latin *veterinae*, cattle.

Horsewomen also weren't taken seriously for a long time. Apart from historic females on horseback like Boadicea in Britain trying to force the Romans out, and Joan of Arc successfully repelling the English in France, women on horses were a rarity of the sort sometimes found in a circus, as many were by the 1800s.

Sidesaddle was designed by men for women, and by the Victorian era it was improper for a lady to ride a horse any other way. One Byzantine princess believed that a female normally astride a stallion could only excite him into an uncontrollable gallop. Barbara Stanwyck, who starred in several film westerns, asserted, "I've ridden both ways, and I grant you, sidesaddle looks graceful, but it's too damned easy to fall off! I got used to it, but I wouldn't willingly choose it for myself."

A palfrey, its name partly from the Latin for light horse, is a docile horse once intended for women to ride. (Unusually, the male stars of TV's long-running western *Bonanza* admitted they were unaccustomed to and uncomfortable on horses.)

Nag is a derogatory term for a horse, especially one that's old or ailing. It originally meant a horse for riding, rather than a draft animal. A mount is also a horse for riding, as is a saddle horse. A dobbin is a draft horse or farm horse (in the 16th century Dobbin was a nickname for Robert).

The other nag, both the verb and the noun attached to a wife who repeatedly asks her reluctant husband to do something, doesn't have an animal origin. Unlike another stereotypical wife, a shrew, named after the mouselike mammal with teeny eyes and no particular temperament that became synonymous with a bad temper, which trait was applied to wives, not husbands.

A mare's nest is an impossibility, so to find one means to make a discovery that proves worthless. One source of the phrase may be a Central European fable about a discontented youth who searches in vain for a magical mare's nest. Regardless, paintings of mare's nests are unique and often fetching.

Horseradish

Grated horseradish root, cream, and vinegar combine into a condiment often considered a must with prime rib or roastbeef. Of course horseradish has nothing to do with horses. Nor is this member of the cabbage family a radish, though in some cultures it was deemed a larger, coarser, more pungent version of same. The first written reference to the plant was in Pliny the Elder's *Natural History*, published in 77–79 CE. The Roman scholar believed it had medicinal value, as many still did in the Middle Ages.

The horse connection may have accrued via an early method of processing the vegetable by crushing it under a horse's hoof. More likely, it's due to an English mistranslation of the plant's German name, *Meerrettig*, or sea radish, since it grew along the coastline. *Meer* (sea) was confused with the English mare (a female horse), resulting in the same type of permanent misnomer as the Pennsylvania Dutch, who were German (*Deutsch*), not Dutch (*Nederlander*) immigrants. Didn't people check these things?

Horseplay

A morris dance is a traditional English dance performed alfresco by groups of dancers holding sticks or handkerchiefs, whose costumes feature small attached bells. At country fairs the dancers were often joined by players on hobby horses— a model of a horse's head, on a long stick. The faux horses entertained the throngs with rambunctious but harmless "horseplay."

Morris derives from Moor or Moorish. Traditional *Othello* casting aside, a Moor is a North African Caucasian, often of mixed Arab and Berber descent, and frequently from Morocco or Mauretania.

Horsing around is typically energetic but basically benign, as befits the equine image (imagine bulling around).

Horseface

Obviously if someone has a horseface they have a longer than usual visage. Horse is usually mentioned, unless the focus is presumed sadness. Example—He: Are you Celine Dion? She: No. He: Then why the long face?

The adjective horsey is often used about long-faced people, particularly actors. For instance Fred Gwynne, best known as Herman Munster but much horsier-looking sans *Munsters* makeup on *Car 54, Where Are You?* He later explained, "My face was my fortune and my curse ... it's made for comedy. Until I got older and could play mean old bastards."

Far more actresses than actors have been described as horsefaced, especially during Hollywood's golden era when older character actresses were prominent. Director George Cukor told this writer that lovable and respected though they were, "Come lunchtime, you almost felt like offering them a feedbag." Edna May Oliver declared, "Being made an equine comparison of is no tragedy if critics aren't alluding to an old nag but, as I like to think of it, a thoroughbred champion. Let them put that in their pipe and smoke it!"

Horsey can also refer to people of means who frequent race tracks, as in the line from Tennessee Williams's *The Glass Menagerie* about "the horsey set on Long Island." That play's symbolism features a crystal unicorn which, accidentally knocked to the ground, loses its horn and becomes like the other horses.

Famous Horses

There has always been a handful of famous horses at any given time. Once, they were those of rulers and military leaders, for example, Alexander the Great's Bucephalus, a virtual companion to the long-roving conqueror. Pegasus, the winged horse of Greek mythology, is another of few equines remembered from ancient times. More recently, there have been racing champions like Secretariat and film-cowboys' steeds like Roy Rogers's Trigger (renowned too for his stuffed afterlife) and the on-screen mounts of characters like the Lone Range (Silver), plus Mr. Ed from the eponymous TV series (Bamboo Harvester was the palomino that played him) and B-movie-series star Francis the Talking Mule.

Cesar Romero, a.k.a. the Joker on TV's *Batman*, was one of several actors who depicted the Cisco Kid (the first, Warner Baxter, won a Best Actor Oscar in the role, in the 1929 film *In Old Arizona*). Romero recalled, "I'm not a great pet lover and riding's not my favorite sport, but in very little time I came to feel closer to my horsey costar than I ever did to any human costar, with one exception…. An animal trainer told me there's a very atavistic relationship between human beings and their horses, which I can well believe."

Writer-director Arthur Lubin, who created both Francis and Mr. Ed, felt, "People take a horse seriously in a way they don't with a smaller animal. When I added speech, audiences reacted exactly as if two people were relating and talking to each other. It's a winning combination!"

The favorite horse of a family named Mars who were in the confectionary business wasn't famous, but in 1930 they named their new candy bar after him. His name was Snickers.

The Horse's Mouth…

Straight from the horse's mouth is firsthand and presumably accurate. The phrase implies provability, as in olden days when a man went to buy a horse. A rare woman might buy a horse, but women were themselves chattel, not allowed to own property or major possessions in their own names. Chattel, which now rhymes with cattle—pronunciation changes more often than spelling—is from the Old French *chatel*, whose Anglo-Norman French variation *catel* yielded the word cattle.

A horse was then as major an expenditure as a car is today, and one didn't want to overspend on an animal with possibly not much work left in it. The chief method of gauging a horse's age was to examine its teeth and see how much they'd worn and how far the gumline had receded.

Don't look a gift horse in the mouth is also from the long period—human history till the twentieth century—when most transportation was equine. It was considered the height of rudeness to check a horse's teeth and therefore its value when the horse was a gift (like asking for the receipt of a present today).

The warning to beware of Greeks bearing gifts derives from Homer's epic *The Iliad*, about the war pitting Trojans against Greeks. In order to get inside heavily fortified Troy—where Helen, originally not of Troy, was—the Greeks built a huge wooden horse in which were secreted several soldiers. The gargantuan equine, standing outside the city gates, intrigued the Trojans, many of whom believed it was sent by the gods. The horse was brought inside, the soldiers emerged, and the rest is, if not necessarily history, a riveting story and a warning to check the contents of a tempting present.

Speaking of a horse's mouth, it's nearly impossible for horses to vomit, due to the acute angle between an equine throat and stomach. Vomiting enables humans to purge sick-making substances, whereas horses often die from colic.

Dark Horse

By the 1500s to keep something dark meant keeping it a secret. But the phrase a dark horse, meaning an unknown quantity or one kept secret, was created by Benjamin Disraeli in *The Young Duke* (1831). The debut novel features a horse race in which both favorites are beaten to the finishing line when "a dark horse which never had been thought of rushed past the grandstand in sweeping triumph."

It was standard practice for owners to hide the potential of promising new horses until the day of the race. The 27-year-old aristocrat's novel led to such animals becoming known as dark horses, regardless of their color. Thirty-seven years later, the writer-politician became Prime Minister and later the first Earl of Beaconsfield—the Disraelis were ex-Jews; non-Christians weren't allowed to stand (run) for Parliament.

Today a dark horse can refer to a person of unknown abilities or one who's kept them to herself or himself and may surprise others.

Horse Words

Horse whisperer was a little-known term for somebody claiming special understanding of equines and an ability to communicate with and soothe them. The book and movie of the same name, TV programs, also dog whisperers, cat whisperers—any kind of whisperer but a hoarse one, for it's a lucrative field—have made this a household phrase. (A planned UK TV series is titled *The Husband Whisperer*.)

Horse opera became a nickname for western movies and then TV series by the 1940s. It's also a sob story, as in "Her whole horse opera sounds like a lie." Within a few paragraphs on page 176 of the paperback of Edna Sherry's 1948 novel

Sudden Fear (later filmed) are four animal phrases, three signifying baloney: a fish tale, horse opera, sounds fishy, plus like a cornered rat.

Horse trading was the sale of a horse or the exchange of two horses. Today horses need not be involved. Because it could take longer to judge the value of a horse than most animals, with more room for cheating on the part of the seller, horse trading was often hard and intense. Horse trades often involved one man giving something besides a horse to even the swap. Likewise, business agreements dubbed horse trades or horse trading frequently involve bargaining and skillful discussion.

Horseflesh represents horses collectively, and a connoisseur of horseflesh makes a good horse trader.

A horse pistol was a larger model that a rider carried at the pommel of his saddle. Pommel, the projecting front part of the saddle in front of the rider, is from the Latin *pomum*, fruit or apple, because of its shape.

Horsehair, from the mane or tail of a horse, is used in padding furniture and was sometimes used in wigmaking.

Horsepower

The term horsepower was coined by James Smeaton in 1724 in the UK. A maker of scientific instruments, he improved the efficiency of steam engines and used "horsepower" to calculate their relative workload capacity. This is often wrongly attributed to James Watt, who was overoptimistic about horsepower force; Smeaton's estimate was closer to its true value. Smeaton, who also improved the efficiency of watermills and windmills, devised the term civil engineer to distinguish what he did from what military engineers did.

Horsepower measures how hard a car engine must work to lift 550 pounds (250 kilograms) one foot (30 centimeters) in one second.

Horseless

So ingrained was the idea of horses as transportation that for some time after automobiles came along they were primarily known as horseless carriages. The combustion engine eventually replaced the horse, marking the end of not only an era, but a way of life for most of human history. (The first car to be powered by an internal combustion engine was designed and built by Karl Benz in 1885.)

The iron horse was long a nickname for a railroad locomotive. As it rolled across the country scattering sparks, it scared not only horses but many people.

An old war horse is or was (more often in Britain) a veteran of various battles who enjoyed reminiscing about them.

A willing horse is someone who so enjoys work that they're willing to do others' work as well.

From the long-lasting strength and reliability of a horse came the term workhorse, to describe a person or machine that performs steadily and efficiently over a long period.

The horse latitudes have been known as such since the 1700s. Situated between the westerlies and the trade winds, these belts of sea and calm air are found in both northern and southern hemispheres.

Horse beans are field beans with bigger than usual seeds, used as fodder.

A horsetail is a flowerless plant that produces spores featuring whorls of narrow leaves that may have reminded someone long ago of whirling horse tails.

Horse chestnuts are deciduous trees with white, pink, or red flowers and nuts called conkers inside a spiny case. *Castanea equina* is Latin for horse chestnut, so named because its fruit was reportedly an Eastern remedy for chest diseases in horses.

Horse mushrooms are edible and large, with creamy white caps.

A horse laugh, typically expressing incredulity or derision, is loud and coarse, which doesn't sound fair or similar to a horse's neigh or whinny.

And horse sense is another name for common sense, which is not all that common. (Mr. Ed would say it's even less common among humans.)

To Flog a Dead Horse

This expression meaning to do something pointless has a nautical origin, specifically in the horse latitudes, located within

30 degrees either side of the equator. Because of the area's weak winds (due to subsiding dry air and high pressure), tall sailing ships requiring strong winds inevitably slowed or even stalled.

The passage could take weeks, even months, by which time most sailors had worked off what they called the "dead horse," advance wages gotten when they signed aboard. However, because seamen were paid by the day, they had no incentive to expend extra effort sailing through the horse latitudes, and so the slowed period was nicknamed flogging the dead horse.

Horse Animals

Horses are such a primary animal in human civilization that various creatures resembling them or parts of them, or involved with horses, bear equine names. To wit, the horse-shoe bat (insectivorous, not a blood-sucker) has a horseshoe-shaped ridge on its nose, while the horseshoe crab has a rounded horseshoe-shaped shell and long tail spine.

Horse mackerel are so named because of an old myth that smaller fish could ride on the mackerel's back over great distances along the eastern Atlantic. "Flying fish" gave rise to many incredible stories.

The sea horse has a head and neck that startlingly suggest the grace and beauty of a horse. The male of this unique species is impregnated by the female, carries the offspring, then delivers them. So what's the difference between female and male sea horses? Simple: she provides eggs, he provides sperm.

A horsefly is a larger fly that plagues horses via the female of the species, which sucks blood and leaves painful bites.

Another menace is the horseleech, large and predatory (both genders). Dwelling on land and in fresh water, it feeds off small invertebrates but also carrion, hence the name: it's often seen attached to equine corpses.

(In pre-auto Istanbul, horses—used primarily as draft animals—were usually overworked until they literally dropped in their tracks, disposed of by the city's packs of wild dogs. After cars came in and the dogs, considered unclean in Islam, had served their purpose, the remaining canines were rounded up, shipped to one of the nearby Princes (sic) Islands, and there disposed of via starvation-induced cannibalism.)

A Bit... of Sleep

Back in 470 BCE the Greek playwright Aeschylus wrote, "You take the bit in your teeth like a new-harnessed colt." The expression evinces enthusiastic determination to perform a task and derives from the metal bar or bit placed in a horse's mouth and attached to the bridle and reins that allows a rider to steer and control the animal. The phrasing is to get or take or have the bit between one's teeth or—more often in North America—to get the bit in one's teeth.

Horses usually sleep standing up, relaxed and without strain, via interlocking bones and ligaments in their legs. Horses can spend a month continuously standing. Being heavy animals with relatively delicate legs, they're not prone to lie down and get up, then down, then up, very often. A major reason to lie down is to scratch an itch against the ground or grass or leaves, etc. In the wild, when horses do lie down to sleep, one horse always remains erect as a sentry.

Seeing a Man About a Horse

Whereas seeing a man about a dog rarely involved a dog, this equine variation on the Victorian expression was typically literal. Someone saying it was usually headed for the races or going to get a tip about a specific horse.

Sometimes seeing a man about a dog did involve canines, especially in late 19th-century America, where coursing meets employing two greyhounds to chase a rabbit to its death were popular. County fairs also made hefty profits with greyhound races. Because the crowds drawn to any sort of animal race inevitably included shady characters, seeing a man about a horse or a dog eventually also implied engaging in any nefarious or illegal activity.

Horse Sayings

When there were horses and carriages, a man in a hurry to get home or wherever else he was going (to see a man about a dog?) might order his coachman, "Don't spare the horses." For some time after automobiles came on the scene, some people facetiously but meaningfully said the same thing to the chauffeur. The expression is now rare even in England.

Hold your horses! This phrase demanding patience goes back a few centuries in England but became widely known in the United States and Australia by the 1940s.

If wishes were horses, beggars would ride—indicates an unfulfillable wish.

To drive a coach and horses through a law/regulation/rule—a British expression meaning to find a very large loophole in it.

To back the wrong horse is less to bet on the wrong horse than to rely on the wrong person, thing, or cause.

A two-horse race is one between only two participants or two with any chance of winning, and now often applies to elections.

To get or climb on one's high horse is to assume a superior or moral tone or attitude.

To frighten the horses is to shock public opinion. British stage actress Mrs. Patrick Campbell (1865–1940) famously declared, "It doesn't matter what you do in the bedroom so long as you don't frighten the horses." In other words, to keep it behind closed doors; the phrase projects human indignation and hypocrisy onto horses!

Someone who rides roughshod over another person is cruel and may inflict the psychological pain that a roughshod horse trampling or kicking somebody would inflict physically, for the horseshoes of roughshod horses bear nails intentionally left protruding to allow extra grip in wet or icy weather.

Horsemen

Chivalry in its archaic sense meant knights, noblemen, and horsemen collectively, all predicated on horses, the word itself evolving from Latin *caballus*, horse. Chivalry is now courteous behavior—which was part of the knight's code—particularly of a man toward a woman.

Cavalier meant a cavalryman or a courteous gentleman. Today it's an improperly unconcerned attitude. It and cavalry also evolved from the Latin horse, as did words in the Latin languages that usually mean both horseman and gentleman. For instance, French *chevalier*, knight, which is also a surname (entertainer Maurice Chevalier). Long ago, a man who could afford to buy and keep a horse was often a knight and automatically a gentleman.

On men's restrooms in Latin America one often sees *Caballeros*, gentlemen as well as horsemen; *caballero* is also used to politely address any given man.

Mangiacavallo is an Italian surname translating to eat horse. The opera *Cavalleria Rusticana* by Pietro Mascagni means rustic chivalry.

In German, knight or horseman doesn't come from horse. Rather, *Ritter* (also a surname, as in actor John Ritter, whose father Tex was a cowboy star) is related to *Reiter*, rider.

In the United States, the word esquire is appended to an attorney's name. In Britain, it can be attached to any man's name as a courtesy; in days of old, an esquire was a young nobleman training for knighthood by attending a knight.

An equerry—from *equus*, also horse—was historically an officer in charge of royal or noble stables, is now an officer of Britain's royal household who looks after not horses but royals. (English actor Anthony Steel once said, "The key difference between us and royals is their ancestors killed far more people than ours ever did.")

Mounted...

The Horse Guards are British mounted squadrons provided from the Household Cavalry for ceremonial—and now touristic—purposes. A dragoon is a member of one of various British cavalry regiments (the verb means to coerce someone into doing something). Historically, a dragoon was a cavalryman armed with a carbine, which weapon was compared to a fire-emitting dragon, the origin of dragoon.

Tantivy is a fast ride or gallop, also an exclamation used as a hunting cry (and the name of a UK book publisher). A more famous hunting cry is "tally-ho," yelled to the hounds by a huntsman upon sighting a fox. It's of unknown origin, and not that different from the Lone Ranger's "Hi-yo, Silver," to his trusty steed from 1933 onwards. (Steed is from Olde English steda, meaning stallion and related to stud.)

A horsewhip is a long whip used to drive and control a horse. Numerous old British films and TV programs feature a scene where a chap angrily informs a usually younger one—who's perhaps been seeing his daughter on the sly—"You should be horsewhipped!" The implication is a stronger-than-usual punishment.

By contrast, a riding crop is a short flexible whip, used to devastating effect on Marlon Brando by Elizabeth Taylor in the movie *Reflections in a Golden Eye* after she finds out he's injured her pet stallion.

Horsesh*t

Many linguists agree there are two reasons "horsesh*t" is considered less rude than "bullsh*t." First, it's much less common and thus somewhat startling to the ear. Second, a horse is a "finer" animal than a bull, which is wilder and has cruder connotations (and is a male animal; "horse" is gender-neutral). In general, Germanic—including English—words, typically shorter and more blunt, are deemed less proper than their Latin equivalents, for example "sh*t" versus "feces." (Or "wart" vs. the classier-sounding "verruca.")

Dancer Cyd Charisse (*The Band Wagon, Singin' in the Rain, Brigadoon*, etc.) often urged her Hollywood contemporaries to use the exclamation "horse waste!"

A seldom-used British expression is "rare as rocking-horse manure" (or sh*t), meaning so rare as to be non-existent.

A 1986 ad for Australia's Qantas airlines apprised potential passengers, "You'll agree a better deal is about as likely as rocking-horse manure."

Horsefeathers

This fanciful term, sometimes two words, signifies sheer non-sense and incredulity. According to the *Historical Diction-ary of American Slang* it's a euphemism for horsesh*t. It was coined by cartoonist Billy de Beck (1890–1942), creator of Barney Google, and was made more popular by the 1932 Marx Brothers movie of the same name. (Four years earlier there was a cartoon titled "Horsefeathers.") Groucho Marx once commented, "If horses had enough feathers, they could fly, and what a mess we'd all be in."

The most famous feathered flying horse is the white beauty Pegasus from Greek mythology. He was born from the blood of Medusa after Perseus decapitated the snake-haired Gorgon (one of three sisters). Pegasus then flew Perseus to the rescue of fair Andromeda, as seen in two versions of the movie *Clash of the Titans*.

Winged mammals were art favorites in the ancient Mid-dle East, including the monumental winged-bull carvings of Mesopotamia, on view at museums in London, Paris, New York, etc. They represented a cross between earthly power and sky travel.

Hungry Horse...

Why "hungry as a horse"? Horses and cows (and bulls, oh, my!) are the largest farm animals, but according to philologist Mario Pei the horse, unlike the cow, is regarded as halfway to a pet. "It accompanies a man on a long ride, reacts more individually to humans ... doesn't give the impression of an eating machine like the cud-chewing cow, and exhibits greater intelligence."

Horses loom large in human thought and comparisons. When one thinks of a voracious appetite, one thinks "hungry as a horse," unless one is out camping, in which case it's "hungry as a bear." As for the unfortunate "I could eat a horse," it proves that the horse resides closer to the human imagination than the cow, even when the cow would be more appropriate.

In dire situations, starving humans have resorted to eating a horse, but only as a last resort. In France, however, horsemeat was long an accepted comestible.

To eat like a horse is to be ravenous (which doesn't derive from raven the bird), as does to eat like a pig, but minus porcine bad manners.

Full of beans and feeling one's oats both connote frisky, happy, and well-fed. Both phrases originally pertained to horses. The Romans used horse beans as fodder, thus an energetic horse—and later a person—was full of beans. Likewise with oats, although to get one's oats is British slang for having sex, and to sow one's wild oats implies wild or promiscuous behavior while young.

Frisky horses are the source of expressions like horseplay and horsing around.

"Horse" is one of several nicknames for heroin, which is said to kick equines into overdrive.

A Stalking Horse

This phrase about exploitive deception dates back to the early 16th century, when a horse was specially trained so a huntsman could walk behind it and sneak close up to his target without it being forewarned. A stalking horse could also be an equine-shaped screen behind which a hunter hid while stalking prey. In time it came to mean any front—usually animal or human—for hiding one's real intentions. Most specifically, per the *Concise Oxford English Dictionary*, it's "a candidate for the leadership of a political party who stands only in order to provoke the election and thus allow a stronger candidate to come forward"—with reference to British politics. Interestingly, stalking horses, like cat's paws, seldom benefit from their own actions.

Hack...

Hack is short for Hackney in East London, where horses were pastured. A hack may be an ordinary horse for riding, as opposed to racing, or a poor-quality or tired-out horse. Or a ride on a horse. Not to mention a taxi or a third-rate writer. (Another hack, a variant of hatch, is the board on which a hawk's meat is served.)

A hackney is either a harnessed light horse with a high-stepping trot or a rented-out horse-drawn vehicle. The obsolete verb to hackney meant to employ a horse for general purposes; it birthed the adjective hackneyed, something overused and no longer original.

A hacking jacket is a riding jacket with slits at the back or side.

Hackles are the erectile hairs on an animal's back which rise when it's frightened or angry. To make a person's hackles rise is to offend or anger them. Or excite them, as in the phrase's first usage, in 1883 by writer Edward Pennell: "I almost saw the hackles of a good old squire rise as he waved his hat and cheered."

A hackle is a long, slim feather on a cock or other bird's neck or saddle. When a rooster's hackle rises, he may be preparing for a fight.

A hackle is also a feather twisted around a fishing fly so its filaments splay out. Or the feathers in a military headdress.

A hackamore is a bridle that places pressure on a horse's nose.

And Hackensack's in New Jersey. 'Nuff said.

Hoofers

The hoof of an ungulate is the horny part of its foot, from Latin *ungula*, hoof. Most often, hoof refers to a horse's foot, though the phrase on the hoof is a euphemism for unslaughtered livestock. A hoofer is a professional dancer, specifically a tap dancer and more specifically one who "dances close to the floor" with little or no arm or body movement. Such dancers can produce a rolling sound resembling a horse's gallop with particular steps and heel drops.

The primary nicknames for Broadway dancers are gypsies and hoofers, the former because they move from show to show, theatre to theatre. Multiple Tony-winner Gwen Verdon explained, "We're hoofers because we so depend on our legs and feet. We're valued for that. We're athletes, as horses are, and all too soon we're put out to pasture. ... Also, it's our own nickname, from way back. *We're* the ones comparing ourselves to workhorses."

Choreographer Jack Cole said, "Since I was a kid, I heard about hoofers. I didn't know what a hoofer was, but it sounded energetic and like someone who could go places." To hoof it also means to walk, rather than ride or drive.

Speaking of hooves and shoes, it was the Romans who came up with horseshoes. Why? The Romans built paved roads, and horses not running free and wild require pedi-protection against hard surfaces.

A Horse of Another Color

In Shakespeare's play *Twelfth Night* (published in 1623), Maria says of her double-entendre scheme against Malvolio, "My purpose is, indeed, a horse of that color." It took time for the amended expression to assume its modern meaning of inaccurate comparisons, e.g., something completely different, akin to comparing apples and oranges. It may also denote one item that doesn't fit in a group, for instance Olmecs, Mayans, Aztecs, and Phoenicians (the latter group not from the Americas … as in some multiple-choice exam questions).

The most famous and vivid example of a horse of another color is the one that literally changes colors as Dorothy Gale and her three pals ride a carriage into the Emerald City in the iconic film *The Wizard of Oz*.

In England, some have tried to pin the origin of this expression onto the White Horse of Berkshire, an archaeological oddity comprising a 374-foot-long outline of a horse formed by trenches in a chalk hillside. Local citizens periodically clear the trenches' weeds, thereby making it "a horse of a different color."

A related phrase references a horse's true colors, meaning not the shade or hue it was born with, but its ability to win a race and show what it's truly made of.

Hobby Horse

Besides being a modeled horse head on a stick for a toy, a hobby horse was a sort of velocipede devised in England in the mid 1600s. One sat on the primitive bicycle and pushed oneself along with the feet. "Hobby" meant a small horse or pony, but because some people so enjoyed this mode of leisure transportation, hobby eventually came to mean what people chose to do during their leisure time.

In Britain especially, hobby horse also denotes one's pet topic or even obsession (for instance, conspiracy-theory buffs). When one is told to get off one's hobby horse—equivalent to a soapbox—it typically means enough already, we've heard all this before. To ride a hobby horse to death is to bore everyone else to tears with it. (One's *bete noire*, black beast in French, is by contrast someone or something one particularly detests, a #1 pet peeve.)

Saddle...

Besides what one puts on a horse to ride it, a saddle is the lower part of the back of a mammal or fowl. To be saddled or burdened with something is, however, applied to humans, not horses. To be in the saddle is to be in charge—sometimes on a charger, historically a horse ridden by a knight or cavalryman.

A saddleback, apart from an architectural feature or a kind of hill, is a wattlebird from New Zealand, black with a reddish-brown back.

Saddlebags attach to a saddle. Now they're also extra fat attached to the hips and thighs.

A saddle horse, like a sawhorse or clotheshorse, is a wooden frame or rack on which saddles are cleaned or stored.

Saddle soap, used to clean leather, ironically contains neat's-foot oil, a euphemism for oil made by boiling the feet of cattle. (Neat is an archaic term of Germanic origin for bovine animals.)

A saddle sore on a horse's back results from a poorly fitting saddle.

Saddle stitch is the stitch of thread or the wire staples one sees in the folds of magazines and booklets. It's also a decorative needlework stitch alternating long stitches above with short stitches below.

A saddle tank is a small steam locomotive with a water tank fitted over the top and sides like a saddle.

Saddle shoes (remember them?) have nothing to do with horses.

What has a saddle to do with steak tartare? The Tartars of Central Asia were horsemen first and last, sometimes spending days at a time on their horses. Thundering across the

Eurasian steppes, they often didn't take time out for lunch, instead placing slabs of beef under their saddles until after several hours' riding they became tenderized. We call it *tartare* because the French word presumably distracts from the fact of eating raw meat.

A Horse Is a Horse, Of Course, Of Course

Many or most august readers (or any other month) know that *hippos* is the ancient Greek word for horse, ergo hippopotamus (river horse, to someone with terrible eyesight), hippocampus (horse field), and so on. And of course August is named after the first Roman emperor, Octavian, who restyled himself Augustus.

But it may be slightly mystifying why Latin had two basic words for horse, *caballus* and the more famous *equus* (partly via the notorious play about blinding horses). From these two words derive nearly all horse-related words and terms in English and the Latin languages (sometimes called Romance languages not because of romance but Rome). Although a Germanic language, English exhibits a much greater Latin influence, one reason being the French (Norman) conquest of England in 1066. In German, for instance, horse is *Pferd* (go pfigure).

Basically, there's the genus *equus* (horse), of which the wild horse, *equus ferus*, is a species. One of its subspecies is today's domesticated horse, *equus ferus caballus*. Two other subspecies are Przewalski's Horse, fortunately reintroduced into the wild after surviving the brink of extinction, and the Tarpan, which did become extinct in the 19th century.

So-called wild horses like the Mustang in the United States and the Brumby in Australia which roam free in herds are feral horses—untamed members of the domesticated *equus ferus caballus*—distinct from truly wild equine subspecies.

Pony...

A pony is a small breed of horse, not a baby horse, as many children think. A pony is also a small glass or measure of alcoholic drink and in Britain was slang for 25 pounds sterling. In the United States the ponies meant racehorses, and to pony up is to pay an amount of money, usually to settle an account.

A ponytail is so named for its resemblance to a horse's tail but sounds more girlish. The simple, youthful hairdo was given a huge boost in the late 1950s by the Barbie doll (itself modeled on a sexy German doll sold mostly to grown men!).

A one-trick pony is someone or something limited to one special feature, talent, or asset.

To travel or go by Shank's pony—also Shank's mare in North America—means to use one's own legs, and was first recorded as Shank's nag in Robert Fergusson's *Poems* in 1785.

Regarding a dog-and-pony show (see the chapter Dogs), philologist Mario Pei explained, "The pony was chosen over the horse in the combination because the sizes (of pony and dog) are nearer equal and in a production meant to impress, the pony is more rare than a horse."

Colt and Filly

A colt is a young male horse, uncastrated, under four years of age. A filly is the female equivalent, but the adjective coltish, meaning energetic yet youthfully awkward in movement or behavior, is more often applied to teen girls than boys. (Filly is usually condescending, revealing less about a girl's manner than the speaker's paternalism.) UK animal behaviorist Barbara Woodhouse offered, "The bond between adolescent girls, often tomboys, and horses is famously fascinating. It is asexual, naturally, yet even so is passionate … the horse often substitutes for a future male or female lover. Repressed sexuality has much to do with this, as with young females' sometimes hysterical aversion toward the harmless but hairy spider, which represents male carnality."

In Britain a colt is also a member, usually male, of a junior sports team.

A coltsfoot is a yellow flower with large leaves that's a member of the daisy family (the plural is coltsfoots, not coltsfeet).

A foal is a young horse, period, via Olde English fola, of Germanic origin and related to filly.

Mule...

People familiar with mules understand the expression stubborn as a mule, a rare instance of a descriptively accurate animal phrase.

A mule is also a hybrid plant or animal, particularly a sterile one, since a mule is the hybrid between a female horse and a male donkey, usually sterile.

The offspring of a male horse and a female donkey is a hinny, which in Scotland and northern England is also a term of endearment, a variation of honey.

Mule deer are North American deer with black tail markings and long ears.

Jackrabbit is an abbreviation of jackass-rabbit, a North American hare, so named because of its long ears, resembling those of a jackass or male donkey.

A mule is a stubborn person. Or a woman's backless slipper, via *mule*, a French word for slipper that also means a female mule (*mulet* is a male mule). A mule is also a two-wheeled lifting trolley or dolly for moving heavy items by one person. More recently, a mule is an illegal-drugs courier.

A spinning mule is a spinning machine that yields yarn on spindles.

A mule train comprises a line of pack mules or a line of wagons drawn by mules. Its driver is inappropriately called a mule skinner.

Mulatto is an obsolete term for someone with one white and one black parent, on the pattern of mule from a horse and a donkey. It's from the Spanish *mulato*, a young mule.

Ass...

The judgmental word asinine comes directly from non-judgmental Latin *asinus*, meaning ass. Related to the horse, an ass brays and has longer ears. Ass may also refer to any donkey or to a stupid person or what a person sits on. For centuries, the ass has been a symbol of stupidity, partly by comparison to its larger, more elegant relative the horse. Swiss zoologist Karl Bregi states, "The intelligence of animals is most often judged by their doing or learning to do what humans want of them. A horse may perform better in a circus than an ass, but yet it sometimes is a question of an animal resisting. Stubbornness is a factor."

The few studies of donkey behavior indicate that they are intelligent and friendly. Regarding the relative intransigence of the horse's smaller cousins, many animal behaviorists feel it reflects a greater degree of self-preservation than the horse displays (more horse sense?).

Dr. Bregi adds that the bias of looksism isn't absent from human judgments of animals. "A horse is useful. It is also an animal for show and status, unlike its equine relatives, who are therefore adjudged less intelligent as well as less attractive." Since the ancient Egyptians, longer ears have often consigned an animal to the category of shorter on brains. In *Thus Spoke Zarathustra,* Nietzsche wrote about wisdom, "But such words are not for long ears."

To make an ass of oneself is to behave in a ridiculous or stupid manner. A horse's ass is someone who behaves stupidly or badly or simply a person one dislikes intensely.

The suffix –ass is a derogatory intensifier, as in smartass or dumbass. Half-assed—half-arsed in Britain—means incompetent or inadequate, as indeed half an ass (of any kind) would be.

Donkey...

A donkey is also a domesticated relative of the horse that brays and has long ears. It too is synonymous with a foolish person. Many pejorative phrases apply to the donkey; seldom are its soulful eyes noted.

Donkey's years means, in Britain, a very long time. Donkey ears are long, and in much of the country "years" and "ears" were and are pronounced the same.

To talk the hind leg off a donkey is to chatter on endlessly (related to talking a person's leg off).

Donkey work is the hard or boringly routine part of any job.

A donkey stool is a low stool on which an artist sits.

A donkey engine is a small auxiliary engine.

Like a carrot to a donkey indicates a strong incentive or inducement.

A donkey jacket, used in Britain, is a heavy jacket bearing a waterproof leather patch over the shoulders. In British football (soccer) a poor or unskilled player is called a donkey; likewise in poker.

A donkey derby is a race between people riding donkeys.

"The Donkey Serenade" (1937) is a catchy, kicky tune composed by Czech-born Rudolf Friml.

A burro is a small donkey employed as a pack animal. A burrito is a Mexican appetizer or entrée, depending on its size, comprising a tortilla enveloping beans and/or minced beef and other ingredients. The name comes from its resemblance to the pack that a burro might carry.

Zebra Stripes...

In Britain this is a pedestrian crossing with white stripes. The British pronounce zebra with a short e, vs. the long American e—the pattern repeats in many words, especially with the vowels e and o. Sir Robert Morley, who played Oscar Wilde on stage and screen, offered, "The drawn-out American sound takes longer, is more forceful, and sometimes is brutal-sounding.... The way you say 'homosexual' makes it sound frightening and quite taboo. We say it more naturally."

Contrary to popular belief, zebras and horses can mate. A zorse is the offspring of a female horse and male zebra. A zonkey or zebrass is produced by a she-donkey and a zebra stallion.

A zebra finch is a small Australian waxbill with a black-and-white striped face.

The question of whether zebras are white with black stripes or black with white stripes is answered: either. The animals' shiny coats dissipate up to 70 percent of the sub-Saharan African sun's heat; however, their black stripes can become hotter than the white ones by up to 50 degrees Fahrenheit.

(One doesn't often see a human riding a zebra because zebras, far more resistant to human commands than horses, aren't domesticated. Why haven't people tried to domesticate zebras? Basically because there are more than enough horses, mules, etc., to go around.)

Similarly to Brits calling it a zebra crossing because of its colors and pattern, they often call a black-and-white police car a panda car.

More Horse Sayings

To put the cart before the horse is how this ancient saying about proper priorities is now said, but originally it was "Don't push the cart before the horse." That's because technically a horse pushes, not pulls, a cart, by pushing at the collar of the harness attached to the cart.

To lock the stable door after the horse has bolted, run away, or been stolen is to take precautions after, not before, an unwanted event.

To "put one's money on a scratched horse" is to gamble with no chance of winning or to bet on a sure failure—or what the other party (or fan of the other team) insists is a sure failure.

"A nod is the same as a wink to a blind horse" signifies that some situations don't call for fine distinctions.

"Horses for courses" indicates sticking to what one knows or does best, and refers to the fact that certain horses ran better on particular courses, for example, a left-hand circuit, a right-hand circuit. (Would a horse that needs glasses do well on any course? The Racing Museum in York, England, displays a pair of bifocals created for a local nearsighted trotting horse.)

"Horses sweat, men perspire, and ladies only glow" was a traditional reproof (later listed in the 1972 book *Nanny Says*) to a child coarse enough to say somebody sweats.

"Wild horses wouldn't drag it out of me." (But a little wheedling might.) Unfortunately, this alludes to a real form of historical torture.

OTHER MAMMALS

Capitalist Cows

The combination of humans and cows probably launched capitalism, whose name comes from Latin *caput*, head. Cows are collectively numbered as head of cattle, and were likely the first property humans owned, once certain breeds of oxen were domesticated. Also, because a cow owner is necessarily less mobile than a horse owner, the domestication and husbandry of cattle was presumably instrumental in the first human settlements (husband was once synonymous with farmer). While horsemen could go rampaging across the plains and steppes, cattle and their hypothetically gentler owners developed fixed communities.

Pecus is a Latin word for cattle. The monetary adjective pecuniary is from Latin *pecunia*, money—even though it sounds like the name of a cartoon she-pig.

Penunze is a German word for money, and the Old High German *feo*, meaning cattle or property, survives in the English word fee.

A cash cow is an established property or product that yields consistent earnings (like this writer's McDonald's stock), while the golden calf was, to Moses's wrath, overly prized by some ancient Israelites. Today a golden calf is a commodity valued or overvalued for its own sake.

A Beef, A Bone, No Bones

It's similar to having a bone to pick, except you don't need another person to have a beef. It didn't always mean a complaint. The 1811 *Dictionary of the Vulgar Tongue* said that to "cry beef" was to give a camouflaging alarm. Due to widespread poverty, London had a vast number of thieves, and the poor usually stuck together by drowning out somebody's cry of "Stop, thief!" with loud repetitions of "Hot beef," to confuse passersby and allow the thief to get away. Obviously the one who had a beef was the victim.

Nowadays to beef is also a verb—to complain (or, in an animal vein, to bitch or carp or grouse).

If there's a bone to pick, there are usually two dogs fighting over it. Sometimes three, keeping in mind the old saying that when two dogs fight for a bone, a third often runs away with it. By the early 1700s, an unsettled dispute was often labeled a bone of contention.

The phrase to "make no bones about something," from the mid 1500s, has a culinary origin. It means getting to the point right away, minus hesitation or restraint. As with a bowl of soup where the bones have been removed, since back then—and in many countries today—the soup bowl included meat bones. Once the bones are removed, the soup can be eaten or swallowed right away, without restraint.

Maverick

Samuel A. Maverick (1803–70) was a Texan cattle-owner who asseverated that he wouldn't brand his calves because it was a cruel practice. So a yearling or any calf that could be separated from its mother became known as a maverick. Of course the non-practice allowed Maverick to claim any unbranded calves he found on the range....

In time a maverick—not branded, thus non-affiliated—came to mean a man unwilling to affiliate with any one political party. The term later expanded to denote a person who's independent-minded, defiantly individual, or unorthodox.

Beef...

Besides being a euphemism for the flesh of a cow, bull, or ox, beef has long signified robust or having substance. Hence a beef tomato or beefsteak tomato is especially large and firm. Beefy means muscular, large, powerful. To beef something up is to give it more substance or strength.

Beef tea is a hot drink made with beef extract, often medicinal.

Beefwood is a hardwood tropical tree with close-grained red wood.

A Beefeater is a Yeoman Warder or Yeoman of the Guard at the Tower of London. The name heralds back to their traditional beef rations, which were bigger than most; originally beefeater was contemptuous slang for a well-fed servant.

Beef Wellington, created to honor Britain's naval hero, is beef encased in pâté and enveloped in puff pastry.

Beefalo is a hybrid of cattle and buffalo.

Beefsteak fungus is a reddish-brown bracket fungus, forming shelflike projections from the trunks of trees, that actually resembles raw beef.

Patterned after cheesecake, beefcake is of recent derivation; each refers to sexy eye candy. Why beef, when most beef comes from cows? One reason is "bullcake" doesn't sound right and is negatively linked to bullsh*t. Also, beefcake sounds better than porkcake or chickencake, etc., and beercake wouldn't make sense.

Classic Cows

Up until modern times, most cultures considered it a compliment to tell a female she had cow eyes. In ancient Greece "cow-eyed" was used to describe Hera, the wife of Zeus, king of the gods. As a prime source of wealth, cows were a highly prized dowry in marital arrangements. Daughters were sometimes given names that expressed bovine hopes, for instance Polyboea—she who has many cows—and Phereboia—she who will bring many cows into the marriage.

The Bosporus, which cuts through Istanbul and divides Europe and Asia, was so named—*bosporos*, ox ford or crossing—because Hera became jealous of Zeus's latest paramour, Io, whom she turned into a white heifer. To add injury to insult, she sent a gadfly to sting the poor cow, who jumped over (not the moon, as in the nursery rhyme) from one continent to the next one. The Ionian Sea was named after Io after she swam in it—eventually she resumed human form.

A respected art form in classical Greece was bucolic poetry—from *boukolos*, herdsman, itself from *bous*, ox. Poems like "The Young Cowherd" by Theocritus in the third century BCE movingly illustrate the demands of duty versus love or pleasure. Cowherds were noted Don Juans, as was Krishna, the Hindu god who famously incarnated as a blue-skinned cowherd irresistible to maidens.

Cow...

Interestingly, a cow that has not borne a calf, or only one, is instead called a heifer. In farm language, a cow has had a minimum of two calves. A cow is also the female adult of various other large mammals, including whales, elephants, and rhinoceroses.

Cowpoke is another name for a cowboy, as is the seldom heard cowman—the former has a freer, more youthful (and cinematic) connotation, though both herd cattle.

Cowpuncher is yet another term for cowboy. In Britain, cowboy also denotes an unqualified or unscrupulous trades-man, as well as someone—a cowboy on the road—who drives recklessly and too fast.

In the United States a cowcatcher is the graphically named metal frame in front of a locomotive that shoves aside obstacles on the line.

A cowlick is a lock of hair that hangs over one's forehead.

A cowpat is a round flat piece of cow dung, often used as fuel or fertilizer and prized in Third World countries.

Cowpox is a viral disease of cows' udders similar to mild smallpox that humans can contract. Mad cow disease is the informal name for BSE, Bovine Spongiform Encepha-lopathy, which fatally affects the central nervous system of cows and is believed related to human Creutzfeldt-Jakob disease.

A cowbird is a dark-feathered American songbird that lays its eggs in other birds' nests (see Cuckoo in the chapter on Non-Mammals). A cowfish is a boxfish named after the hornlike spines on its head.

Cowbane, as its name implies, is poisonous, a tall plant found in wet habitats that's a member of the parsley family, as is cow parsley, a hedgerow plant with fernlike leaves bearing big lacy heads of miniscule white flowers.

Cowberry is a low-growing evergreen shrub producing dark red berries.

Cowslip is a wild primula with bunches of fragrant drooping yellow flowers in spring.

Cow parsnip is another name for hogweed, a big white-flowered weed that's also a member of the ubiquitous parsley family (the dissimilar parsnip is also parsley-related).

Elsie

One of the longest-lasting, most popular commercial animal mascots is Elsie the cow, introduced by Borden in 1936 and still wearing a daisy-chain collar. In 1939 Borden had an exhibit at the New York World's Fair that spotlighted its new rotolactor, a rotating milking platform. To gauge the exhibit's popularity, Borden tabulated the questions asked by fair attendees. They found only twenty percent of questions were about the milking machine. Sixty percent asked where Elsie was. Elsie soon appeared in the film *Little Women*, then was given a mate named Elmer. For years Elmer served as background for Elsie, until Borden introduced a white glue made from milk by-products which they felt shouldn't be advertised by Elsie. So they recruited Elmer and called the product Elmer's Glue.

(The difference between skim and nonfat milk? None. By law both must contain less than half a percent milkfat content. When Elsie produced the milk, it included three to four percent butterfat content.)

Bovine Expressions

"Holy cow!" The ejaculation was most widespread in the 1960s, in large measure because of TV's twice-weekly *Batman* series—Robin the Boy Wonder habitually blurted out "holy" exclamations—likewise comedians, hippie usage, and song lyrics (example: "If They Could See Me Now" from *Sweet Charity*). The Batman and Captain Marvel comic strips had featured the expression prior to that, and there were and are variations like holy cats and holy mackerel. Psychologist Betty Berzon explained, "Given a choice between similar animal phrases, most people tend to pick the one with the largest animal, the better to impress."

Since the 1800s, to say I'm all behind like the cow's tail means that one is behind in one's work or tasks. A cow's tail is also, especially in Britain, someone who's behind the others, for example, "Dave was the cow's tail at the exam."

To wait till the cows come home indicates a very long time, for cows, unhurried creatures, take their own sweet time. (The similar a coon's age, dating back to the early 1800s, referred to the mistaken notion that raccoons lived a very long time.)

To have a cow, that is, to become highly agitated or upset, often heard as the negative order "Don't have a cow!" derives from the whimsical notion that bad enough news or information may cause trauma or pain equivalent to giving birth to a cow (a calf).

To kill the fatted calf alludes to the biblical story of the prodigal son and denotes lavish hospitality and forgiveness, usually after a long absence from home.

"Cowabunga!" Though some sources try to assign a bovine origin to this exclamation repopularized in the 1990s by the Teenage Mutant Ninja Turtles, it began life as Kawabonga (sic)—English tends to transform K into C—a signature phrase of Chief Thunderdud on TV's *The Howdy Doody Show*. In the '60s the phrase was adopted by *Gidget*'s surfers as a cry of exhilaration atop, literally, a cresting wave. In the 1970s the phrase moved into *Sesame Street*'s neighborhood.

Calves

Calf, the back of one's lower leg, evolved from Old Norse *kalfi*, leg. Calf, the young bovine, evolved from Germanic *kalam*, little cow (calf also refers to the young of certain large mammals like elephants). In English, both became calf. A calf is also a floating chunk of ice separated from its mother iceberg.

Mooncalf now means a dumb or foolish person and seldom is heard (it's a discouraging word). W. C. Fields in *The Bank Dick* admonishes a bank teller to not be a mooncalf by passing up a good investment opportunity. Originally a mooncalf was the abortive fetus of a cow or other farm animal. Partly influenced by bias against former moon goddesses— the sun was almost invariably male, the moon female— Europeans long believed that the moon had a sinister influence, hence a mooncalf. Eventually the word was applied to anything monstrous. In *The Tempest* (published 1623) Shakespeare calls Caliban a mooncalf. It took centuries to water the term down to mean a dummy (or dodo).

Holy Cow, Sacred Cow

India's "holy cow" is not so much sacred as highly esteemed, not worshipped but revered as a source of food and a symbol of life. Cows are not to be killed, and in the countryside where most families own at least one dairy cow, it's usually treated as a family member. Its milk, curds, ghee butter, urine, dung— all are used, including in religious rites. However, in Indian cities cows are often neglected and scrawny, eating what they can find, sometimes in the gutter.

An annual cow holiday is called Gopastami (don't stick an R in it; pastrami is corned beef!), during which cows are washed and decorated in the local temple and offerings made in hopes that the cow's gifts will continue through the coming year.

McDonald's of India does not sell beef or pork (the latter forbidden to the Muslim minority). Chicken is on the menu at the golden arches, but the company is opening new all-vegetarian outlets to accommodate the nation's 500 million or so vegetarians.

Prime Minister Indira Gandhi explained, "The cow is not only a national symbol, she represents qualities we value, including peace and good neighborliness." Cows also represent reproduction; India, one of the two nations with a billion-plus population, looks set to out-populate China in the foreseeable future, thanks partially to China's one family/one child policy.

In contrast to a holy cow, a sacred cow is not only not held in high esteem, it's denigrated. Of course it's a symbol, seldom bovine and seldom female, and typically is invulnerable to change. For instance, an excessive military budget is criticized by many as a sacred cow. The phrase is almost always used in the negative and is in part a sarcastic reflection on holy cow.

Hide...

To say one will tan or whip someone's hide is also to demean them via use of the word for an animal's skin. To save somebody's or one's own hide implies a rescue or escape fraught with difficulty. To see neither hair nor hide of somebody is to not see them at all. Some literary authorities believe Robert Louis Stevenson chose the name Hyde for the violent alter ego of the good Dr. Jekyll because of its animalistic implications. On the other hand, there's London's estimable Hyde Park....

The US term tan for suntanned human skin originated with tanning, converting hides into leather by soaking them in liquid that contains tannic acid, which has nothing to do with the potent tanna leaves in old mummy movies. The acid, also known as tannin, is found in some barks (not the canine kind!) and galls. Another meaning of gall—resentment or a skin-sore from chafing—comes from Olde English gealle, the sore on a horse.

Hidebound has an interesting history. It means to be stuck in or limited by tradition and old-fashioned ideas. In the 1500s it referred to malnourished cattle, later also to emaciated humans and from thence the current sense of a thin or narrow outlook.

Diner Lingo

The 1930s through the '50s were the golden age of the American diner, also known as a lunch house or hash house. Waitresses and countermen developed a specialized lingo for more efficient ordering, some of which one's heard in old movies. A few terms went mainstream, such as o.j. for orange juice, b.l.t. for a bacon, lettuce, and tomato sandwich, mayo for mayonnaise, and over easy and sunny side up for particular egg styles.

Some contemporary diners have revived the lingo in an attempt at nostalgia. Here are some examples of that not-quite-dead language:

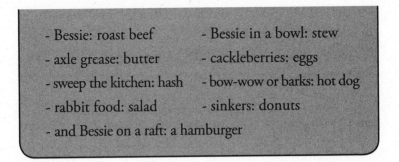

- Bessie: roast beef
- Bessie in a bowl: stew
- axle grease: butter
- cackleberries: eggs
- sweep the kitchen: hash
- bow-wow or barks: hot dog
- rabbit food: salad
- sinkers: donuts
- and Bessie on a raft: a hamburger

Milk...

In Shakespeare's *Macbeth* (published 1623), Lady Macbeth chides her murderous but faltering husband for being "too full of the milk of human kindness." With its pure whiteness and nourishing qualities, milk has been equated with goodness, health, and plenty by several cultures. Note the ancient Israelites' promise of a "land flowing with milk and honey." In some places in medieval Europe, if a body were thought possessed by a demon or devil, milk was poured over them to purify their soul.

A companion of Rudyard Kipling reported back to a Scottish friend that in one district of southern India the pious custom was to forsake all pleasure while mourning the dead, particularly drinking milk. So, one of the worst local insults was to tell somebody, "I will drink milk when you die!"

A milky complexion remains desirable, but in centuries past it was sometimes thought to be attainable by bathing in milk—on the same principle as you are what you eat (in which case a large percentage of Americans would say "moo" regularly).

Milch—milk in German, *Milch*—is the English word denoting any domestic mammal kept for giving milk, while a milch cow is an individual or organization that's an easy and plentiful source of profit or benefit.

Besides milking a cow or other animal, one can milk a situation (milk as plenty). When this writer's sister heard that a blonde costar from a 1970s TV sitcom had recently written a memoir about the series, she observed, "She really knows how to milk it."

Does warm milk really induce sleep? It seems to in some people; however, studies reveal that the biggest factor is whether one *believes* it will (mind over mattress).

Riding Herd

Originally it was a cowboy who would ride herd on cattle, keeping them together and moving in his intended direction. The implication was assuming control, pushing the cattle to where the cowboy wanted them to go, rather than letting them be. After even the once-wild west became urbanized, "riding herd" became associated with perhaps excessive supervision, typically in an office and by a boss.

The term now usually applies in a business or government context, for instance, someone riding herd on a project or department under his or her control. Those being ridden are seldom comfortable with the fact—or the pressure, for instance, "She always rides herd on us during inventory week." A much newer verb comparable to riding herd, especially when the supervision is too close, is "micromanaging." (Which a cowboy might have associated with microbes.)

The associated "riding close herd," or keeping the cattle close together, could now refer to a boss from hell, one who fixes a close, careful eye on someone.

International Cows

In the United States, which long remained more agricultural than England, cow isn't a pejorative term for a woman. Unexpectedly, to cow somebody is to intimidate them. The femaleness of cows is less emphasized in North America. For instance, to have a cow, meaning to become angry or excited, is gender-neutral. However, stupid cow or selfish cow is a frequent feminine put-down in Britain. In Australia and New Zealand, cow can mean any unpleasant person or thing.

Vache, French for cow, can be a disliked female or anything nasty. Where one might exclaim "Holy cow!" in English when taken by surprise, in French one says "*La vache!*" (The cow!) about the unexpected.

One of the most popular breakfast or snack foods in continental Europe is the small wedges of soft processed cheese in a round cardboard container called *La Vache Qui Rit*, The Laughing Cow.

In German, to say "One takes the cow with the calf" denotes a man marrying a woman who already has a child. In several European languages, to "Chew the cud" signifies either thinking something over or talking it out with someone (German for to chew is *kauen*). *Kuhhandel*, literally cow trade, can denote a shady deal, inasmuch as it takes longer to find out how well a cow performs than most animals.

Cattle

Comparing industrial workers to cattle was common by the 19th century, by which time it was clear that despite its positives the Industrial Revolution had robbed many people of choice, decision-making, creativity, and any motivation but money enough to eat. When director Alfred Hitchcock much later said that actors were cattle he meant his brand of highly pre-planned moviemaking eliminated what actors normally do under more spontaneous circumstances, including making their own creative choices.

A cattle call is an open audition for roles in a TV program, ad, film, or more likely a play or musical, often open even to non-union members, with potentially hundreds of thespians showing up for a handful of parts.

A cattle chute forcibly guides cattle to where their owners want them to go. For humans, it's a confined and directed line, for example, tourists queuing up to view the Mona Lisa at the Louvre in Paris. (Many chutes slope or slide; human ones almost never.)

A cattle prod is a cruel device with an electric charge, used to maneuver cattle from a chute into the truck that takes them to the slaughterhouse—*abbatoir* in French, from the verb meaning to fall, as many individual cattle stumble and fall in such jam-packed conditions or are hit over the head and made to fall. (Consider reading *No Happy Cows* by John Robbins, the Baskin-Robbins heir whose bestsellers include *Diet For a New America*.)

A cattle egret is a small egret or huron that usually feeds around grazing cattle.

A cattle grid, more often called a cattle guard in North America, is a metal grid that covers a ditch and enables pedestrians and vehicles but not animals to go across.

Ruminating

When humans ruminate, they ponder something deeply. When cows do it, they chew their cud. A ruminant is an even-toed ungulate mammal which chews its cud, including cattle, sheep, deer, antelopes, giraffes, and related species. A ruminant may also be a person given to meditation. The Latin *ruminari* is to chew over again, and rumen (Latin for throat) is the name of the first of a ruminant's four stomachs—the one that receives the food or cud, digests it partially, then passes it into stomach #2. (Aren't you glad humans have only one!)

Running Bulls

The annual running of the bulls in Pamplona, Spain, began in 1852 as part of the nine-day festival of San Fermin, usually in July. In 1998 Mesquite, Nevada, initiated its own version of the taurine event, with runners paying $50 apiece to be chased by twenty 1,500-pound Mexican fighting bulls through a narrow course the equivalent of six football fields.

On September 28, 2013, there was a running of the bulldogs at Caesars (sic) Palace in Las Vegas, a race to publicize the hotel's Pet-Stay program (despite its name, dogs are the only welcome pets). First to cross the finish line and take home a package of treats was a speedy non-beauty named Lola (her owners got a two-night hotel stay).

Lily Livered

Ancient Greeks customarily sacrificed a major animal such as an ox or bull on the eve of battle. Like their successors the Romans, they saw omens in slaughtered animals' entrails. If the pre-battle sacrifice's liver was red and bloody, that was a positive omen; if pale and lily-colored, negative. The Greeks believed that cowards' livers were pale and lily-colored.

Non-Bulls

A bull market is one in which share prices are rising. To be bullish or bull pro the stock market is to confidently buy shares expecting later to sell at a profit (see Bear further on in this chapter).

To be bullheaded is to be obstinate and unreasoning. A man with a bullneck has a strong thick one.

A bulldozer is named after the animal with a powerful, determined shove.

A papal bull has nothing to do with taureans, nor does—though it would be a good guess—a bully, which began in the 1500s as a term of endearment to a male friend.

Taurus is the second sign of the zodiac and also the constellation the Bull, named after one tamed by the mythical Greek hero Jason (he of the Golden Fleece).

Taurine is an amino acid containing sulphur that's key to the metabolism of fats. Its name owes to its originally being extracted from ox bile.

A bullhorn is, in North America, a megaphone.

A bull bar is a strong metal grille on the front of a motor vehicle that protects against impact damage (similar to a cowcatcher on a train).

A bullpen is an exercise area for baseball players or a holding area where prisoners are held before a court hearing.

A bull fiddle is a double bass, a bullwhip has a long heavy lash that loudly cracks the silence, and a bulrush or bullrush is one of various waterside plants, from "bull"—large or coarse.

Bull-nosed denotes a rounded edge or end. A bull ring, vs. a bullring where bullfights occur, is placed in a bull's very sensitive nose, for a rope, to lead and control him. If the bull is especially aggressive, a halter may also be used. (By the way, bulls have been known to carry a grudge.) Cows very rarely require a ring or halter, having much milder dispositions than their bull-headed mates.

A bull session involves a group of people—sometimes all-female—talking about something.

A bull's-eye is the center of the target in archery and darts, also a big peppermint-flavored candy. It used to mean a small round window in a ship; in French, *oeil de boeuf* (bull's eye) is still a round window, not necessarily small, and usually on a building's upper story.

Chief Sitting Bull was the spiritual leader and tribal chief of the Hunkpapa Lakota Sioux who resisted repressive US government policies against his people, including concentrating them in camps or "reservations."

No Flies On You

This expression goes back to cattle ranching in the USA and Australia and was first noted in the mid 19th century. Plainly put, individual cattle and horses that were more active and mobile than their sedentary counterparts attracted fewer flies.

Caution: In some cultures, to tell individuals they have no flies on them, though meant as a compliment, is apt to be taken as impertinent or insulting. Interesting and sad that the worse a society treats animals, the more apt its people are to be insulted by animal expressions and comparisons. Mahatma Gandhi pointed out that the degree of a nation's moral generosity parallels its treatment of animals.

Bull Critters

A bullock is a castrated male raised for beef, but a bullhead is a small fish with a wide flattened head and spiny fins—or an American freshwater catfish (go figure).

A bullfrog is a very big frog with a deep, resounding croak. A bull snake is a big constricting North American serpent. And a bull ant is a big Australian ant with a powerful sting and large jaws.

A bull terrier is a cross between a bulldog and a terrier, while a bull trout is simply a North American trout found in cold rivers and lakes.

A bullfinch is a stocky bird with mostly black and gray feathers and a white rear; the male boasts a pink breast.

The forerunner of tauromachy or bullfighting was the ancient Cretan sport of bull jumping, practiced by acrobatic young people of both sexes who often literally took the bull by the horns, then vaulted over it.

Gravy

"Gravy" may come from the mistaken reading of a French word derived from the Latin *granum*, or grain. It means both the fat and juices exuded from cooking meat and the sauce made from same. It became slang for easy or found money, while a gravy train is an easy way to make lots of money. In the first half of the 20th century, to board the gravy train and board the gravy boat were popular phrases; an actor in the 1940s stated, "Once you get on the Hollywood gravy boat, it is no trick to make money."

Today the surviving expression is to ride the gravy train. According to linguistics PhD Rosemarie Ostler, since the 1880s the expression has meant "to gain an undeserved benefit or achieve something at the expense of others."

Gravy may also refer to freebies or extra benefits, the extra often summed up with "The rest is gravy."

P.S. Barbecue comes from the Spanish *barbacoa*, one of countless corruptions of a Native American word, in this case via the Arawaks of the Caribbean whose word meant a wooden grill for cooking meat. (Like the Caribs and other tribes of the region, the Arawaks are virtually extinct.)

Bullish Expressions

To be like a bull in a china shop—something seen literally only in movies—is to act clumsily, tactlessly, or destructively in a delicate situation.

"Like a bull at a gate" means hasty, thoughtless, and overly forceful.

To "hit the bull's-eye" is to achieve one's exact aim or attain a great success or make the correct decision.

To "be within a bull's roar" of something is to be very close to something.

To be a "red rag or flag to a bull" signifies something that makes someone very angry or excited, via the incorrect belief that bulls go mad because of the color red rather than the motion of waving.

To "shoot the bull"—or the breeze—originated in the United States and means to have a casual conversation.

"Bull" is criminal slang for a policeman or prison guard.

"Bullsh*t" is a strong word for nonsense because it references a strong animal.

Horns

To take the bull by the horns (just try it!) is to deal effectively with a tough or unpleasant situation. To be on the horns of a dilemma indicates a choice between two unpleasant alternatives and not being sure which is less negative. To draw in one's horns may refer to deciding to spend less money or drawing back from a situation and pondering it before taking action. This expression may derive not from bulls but from snails, which have an eye on the tip of each horn. When a snail senses danger or feels threatened, it withdraws its horns and then its whole body into its shell (during times of drought, snails, which require moisture, may stay in there for weeks at a time).

Ox...

Because of its size and strength, the ox long ago became something of a symbol for brute strength and lack of intelligence, as in expressions like "You big ox" and "You dumb ox." (Female oxen are seldom referenced.)

Oxtail soup is still popular in some quarters and was once believed to lend the consumer some of an ox's strength.

Ox tongue is both the animal's tongue used as meat and a member of the daisy family with prickly hairs and yellow dandelion-like flowers.

Oxlip is a woodland plant with dependent yellow flowers. It's a member of the primula family that includes primroses, cowslips, and polyanthuses. A false oxlip is the hybrid of a primrose and a cowslip.

An ox-eye daisy has big white flowers with yellow centers.

An oxpecker isn't what you think, but a brown African bird related to starlings that feeds on parasites infesting the skins of big grazing mammals.

An oxbow is the U-shaped collar of an ox's yoke, also the loop in a river created by a horseshoe bend. An oxbow lake is curved via a horseshoe bend in a river that no longer flows around the bend in the main stream's loop. (Curiously, the classic 1942 film *The Ox-Bow Incident*, about lynching in the Old West, starring Henry Fonda, was renamed *Strange Incident* for the British market.)

First a Saxon military site, later home to one of the world's leading universities, Oxford, England, was named after a ford where oxen routinely crossed. Back then (ca. 900 CE) bridges were much rarer than fords—shallow places in streams or rivers that could be crossed on foot or in a usually horse-drawn vehicle.

Olly, Olly, Oxen Free, the name of a children's game akin to Hide and Seek, never had a thing to do with oxen. It's an English corruption of its German name: Alle, Alle, Auch Sind Frei—meaning Everyone, Everyone, Is Also Free.

Chewing the Fat

Today, "chewing the fat" refers to casual conversation or gossip. But in the 1800s it was British slang for grumbling or complaining (the related "chewing the rag" is now obsolete). After the expression arrived in North America it took on the more positive meaning of chatting informally.

Originally, the chewing wasn't necessarily verbal and could indicate someone forming words while thinking of something else. As in Shakespeare's *Measure for Measure* (published 1623), wherein Angelo cites his habit of mouthing empty prayers: "… heaven in my mouth,/As if I did but only chew his name,/And in my heart the strong and swelling evil/Of my conception …."

A cow chewing her cud can parallel someone chewing fat, tobacco, or gum. Further American slang featuring chewing includes: to chew over an idea, to chew someone out, and the practically extinct chewing match, which in the 1950s and '60s meant a loud argument.

There's also to "chew somebody's ear off," as in "yak-yak-yak," which has nothing to do with a yak (the large, shaggy ox), whose name comes from the Tibetan *gyag*.

More literally, among the Inuit (formerly, Eskimos) idle hours were sometimes spent chewing animal hides in order to soften them. (FYI, muktuk is the skin and blubber of a whale, eaten as food by the Inuit. Flense is a rarely heard verb meaning to slice the skin or fat from a whale.)

Bringing Home the Bacon

In England in the Middle Ages (till about the 15th century), pork was not only the most commonly available and relatively affordable meat, it was for most people the only meat they ever partook of. But pre-electricity and refrigeration, storage was a problem. Less so with bacon, whose smoking and salting process meant it didn't have to be eaten right away. One side of bacon could suffice a family an entire season. And a small bit of bacon made pease much more palatable. (The latter, made from yellow split peas, was for centuries the staple of the average English diet; the omnipresent meats seen in period films were reserved for royalty and the nobility.)

In the pre-Independence American colonies pork was rare—pigs were introduced to the Americas from Europe—so the Native American who could "bring home the bacon" was a man of means. To show off his status, he would invite some male friends to visit and literally chew the fat.

In Britain and the States, rural contests involving catching a greased pig or excelling at some sport or show of strength often yielded a prize pig to the winner, who—what else—brought home the bacon. Oink, oink.

Hamming It Up

This expression comes from "ham-fatter," which first appeared in 1879 in *America Revisited* by George Sala, who wrote, "Every American who does not wish to be thought 'small potatoes' or a 'ham-fatter' or a 'corner loafer' is carefully 'barbed' and fixed up in a hair-dressing salon every day." In other words, if a male—every *other* American—didn't wish to be thought a nobody, low-class, or unemployed, he went to a barbershop (daily, yet).

Like other performers, musicians were deemed low-class. They were nicknamed ham-fatters because trombone players often kept a piece of ham fat handy to grease their instruments. (A popular minstrel song was titled "The Ham-fat Man.")

By the 20th century, ham fat had shortened to ham and signified a second-rate actor or a vaudevillian. Later in the century it came to include overly dramatic performances ("hamming it up") and productions. As in Raymond Chandler's 1942 novel *The High Window*: "Don't feed me the ham. I've been in pictures. I'm a connoisseur of ham."

A 1970s British print ad for ham converted the landmark "Hollywood" sign to "Hammywood," and actor Dudley Moore said Sir John Gielgud called Laurence Olivier, who relished acting in false noses and accents and often accepted big money for grade-B Hollywood projects, Sir Ham-on-Rye.

Today being a ham covers any type of showing off, thespic or otherwise.

Hams

Besides the primary culinary meaning and secondary one of over-obvious actors, hams are the back of the human thigh or the buttocks and thighs. Hammy describes a thick, solid hand or thigh. Ham-fisted means clumsy or awkward, via large hands (alluding to sizeable pre-sliced hams) and thick fingers.

The hamstring is the large tendon behind a quadruped's hock; hamstrings are the five tendons at the back of a human knee. To hamstring somebody is to cut their hamstrings or, less gruesomely, to thwart or severely restrict someone.

A radio ham is an amateur radio operator. Hambone usually describes a hammy actor.

Ham (and the obsolete hom) comes from Olde English, referring to the back of the knee and based on a Germanic root meaning to be crooked.

Deviled Ham

The William Underwood Company was a leading food supplier to Union troops during the US Civil War (1861–1865). In 1868 the company's kitchen combined ground ham with mustard, cayenne pepper and other spices, in a process called deviling. In 1870 Underwood patented its red devil logo, now the oldest food trademark in the United States. To cook something with hot spices was to devil, a long-established if not widely popular method of preparation, as spices were luxury items.

Dr. Johnson's official biographer, James Boswell (1740–1795), described his passion for "deviled bones," apparently a supper of spicy spare ribs.

Swine

Swine, from the Germanic *swin*, related to sow, doesn't have the same negative connotation in Britain as in the States, where to call someone a swine is worse than calling them a pig, which doesn't usually have moral implications.

Philologist Mario Pei explained, "Swine versus pig is an example of an equivalent word taking on unwarrantedly dark associations. With a pig we associate jollity, excessive love of eating, and down-to-earthiness.... The long I in swine, contrasting with the short i in pig, gives that word a nastier edge."

To cast one's pearls before swine is to waste what is worthwhile on those who won't appreciate it (similar to caviar to the general, that is, general public). The Bible warns, "Do not give what is holy to dogs; nor cast your pearls before swine lest they trample them under their feet, and turn and tear you to pieces."

Swine fever is an intestinal viral illness of pigs. Swine flu is a type of porcine influenza and a human influenza caused by a virus, with notable outbreaks in 1976 and 2009. The former flu is rarely transferred from pigs to humans.

Going the Whole Hog

"The Love of the World, or Hypocrisy Detected" was a 1779 poem by William Cowper in which he described Muslim leaders trying to figure out what part of a hog was edible

(Muslims and Orthodox Jews are enjoined against eating pork). "But for one piece they thought it hard, from the whole hog to be debarred." It was the first print reference to "whole hog."

"Going the whole hog," denoting a strong commitment, was a slogan in Andrew Jackson's 1828 run for president. It was the first campaign involving ordinary Americans rather than aristocrats. Jackson defeated incumbent Federalist John Quincy Adams by stressing government by the average man rather than a political elite. In 1832, he again campaigned with "Go the whole hog!" and was reelected. His followers created the modern Democratic Party.

An 1852 book titled *Household Words* noted, "When a Virginia butcher kills a pig, he is said to ask his customers whether they will 'go the whole hog'… in such case, he sells at a lower price than if they pick out the prime joints only." In pre-refrigeration days, a whole hog, ca. 200 pounds, was a serious commitment.

Another meaning for whole hog derived from the slang "hog," a British shilling or American dime. At the time, most non-millionaires would have deemed it reckless to spend a whole shilling or dime at once. Variations on going the whole hog included to proceed the whole pork, go the entire swine, go the entire animal, or just "go the whole." Current usage typically drops "the," such as "She's going whole hog for self-improvement."

Living High on the Hog

The most in-demand, expensive cuts of a hog (e.g., roasts and chops) are located high on its body, hence a bigger income is required to live high on the hog (a phrase that may have created more than a few vegetarians). Average people have traditionally consumed the rest of the hog, from its feet to the ears, tongue, and brains.* In 19th-century America pigs were easily the nation's #1 meat source (cows were more expensive to raise and transport).

Americans in the 1800s ate a surprising quantity of salt pork, which kept well and was more practical for those living in isolated regions—also for travelers. European visitors of the period often commented that Americans seemed to exist mostly on meat.

Variants of living high on the hog include living high off the hog and eating high off the hog. With the trend toward healthier eating—specifically, less mammal meats—the popularity of hog expressions has tapered off.

*The brains of pigs and calves, pressed with jelly, are made into headcheese, called brawn in Britain, derived from a Germanic word meaning the fleshy part of the leg. Primitive cultures often believed ingesting brains increased one's intelligence. A tribe of New Guinea cannibals in the 1900s found out otherwise, reserving human brains for consumption by women and children (apparently the men thought themselves smart enough). It was a no-brainer to figure out why women and children soon after started dying off.

Hog...

Hog has become synonymous with greedy, and "to hog" is to take more than one's fair share or to hoard. Road hogs take up more than their share of the road. Hog-wild is a North American expression meaning overly enthusiastic.

Hogwash now means nonsense but when originated in the 1400s it was kitchen swill to feed the pigs. (Until fairly recently, the French considered corn more fit for porcine consumption than people's—odd, in a nation that doesn't mind ingesting snails, frogs, and horsemeat!)

A hogfish is a big, brightly colored fish—with thick lips and strong teeth—mostly found in the western Atlantic. A hognose snake is a non-venomous burrowing American snake with an upturned snout. When frightened, it becomes inflated, thereby presumably frightening the other party.

In Britain, a hogg (sic) is a sheep before its first shearing and a hogget is a yearling sheep. A hogget in New Zealand, which has far more sheep than people, is a lamb between weaning and its first shearing.

Hognut is another name for earthnut, which isn't a nut, but a plant related to parsley with an edible roundish almond-flavored tuber (almonds aren't nuts either, but members of the rose family).

Hogweed is also a member of the parsley family. A weed with big white flowers, it was used as forage for pigs.

Pig's Eye, Pigs Fly

The first record that pigs have small eyes for their size, the opposite of cats and human babies, was in the 1500s. Strange that it took so long to write it down, though countless documents disintegrated through time and countless others were destroyed by conquering cultures. Symbolically, the porcine eye was too small to hold much imagination or human warmth, as in poet Richard Flecknoe's "Enigmaticall (sic) Characters" (1658): "She have (sic) the spirit in her of twenty school-mistresses, looking with her Pigs-eyes so narrowly to her charge."

By the 1800s Americans had changed the meaning of *in a pig's eye* to incredulity. (A modern equivalent is "No way!")

An alternative already existed; in 1732 Thomas Fuller wrote in *Gnomologia*, "That is as likely as to see a Hog fly." (In olden days English nouns were often capitalized, as they still are in German.) Another rejoinder to a fantastical statement was "And pigs might fly" or "When pigs fly."

Why air-borne pigs, of all animals? Pigs and hogs are associated with *terra firma*, wallowing in mud, rooting in the earth, plus they're stocky. Easier to picture a cat soaring upward, with its lighter frame, greater poise, and talent for balletic leaps and survived falls from high places. Perhaps simply because flying pigs are harder, and funnier, to picture.

Hog II...

In 2006 Harley-Davidson Inc. changed its NYSE listing from HDI to HOG. The company had unsuccessfully sued H.O.G., a Harley Owners Group club, and attempted to copyright "hog," but an appellate panel ruled in 1999 that the word had become a generic term for large motorcycles. It started in the 1920s when a group of farm boys calling themselves the Hog Boys often won races on their Harley-Davidsons. Their mascot was, depending on the source, a hog or a small pig, and after each win the animal would be put on the motorcycle and taken for a victory lap.

Of unknown origin, a hogshead can be a large cask or a liquid measure for wine or beer, differing in its US, imperial (British), and metric proportions.

Hogback or hog's back is a long, steep hill or mountain range.

To hog-tie is a North American term for securing an animal or human by fastening all four feet or the hands and feet together. It also means to significantly impede.

Hogmanay, New Year's Eve in Scotland, has aught to do with hogs or pigs. It may derive from Norman French meaning the last day of the year or a new year's gift.

To Eat Like a Pig

To eat like a pig is self-explanatory, but did you know German has two verbs for "to eat": one for humans, one for animals. Thus in German one needn't specifically reference a pig or hog to indicate that a human eats greedily and sloppily; one simply uses the alternate verb form.

Likewise Spanish has separate words for the legs of humans versus animals, so a person's thick legs may be described as *patas* instead of *piernas*. (In Japan, thick legs are "radish legs." Go figure.)

As for someone having "the manners of a pig," that doesn't make much sense, for manners, per the *Concise Oxford English Dictionary*, are "polite or well-bred social behavior," and pigs—hogs too—have no awareness of being polite or well-bred, whether eating or wallowing in mud.

Pig Expressions

The word pig likely derives from Olde English picbred, meaning an acorn but literally pig bread (i.e., food for pigs). A pig is also an oblong piece of iron or lead from a smelting furnace or a close-fitting device in an oil or gas pipeline that's sent through it to clean or test the inside or provide a barrier.

A pig in a poke—poke being a bag—is something bought sight unseen or untested.

The British phrase a pig of a (blank) has largely been superseded by the American-influenced a bitch of a (blank), as in "I've had a pig of a day, don't ask."

On the pig's back is Irish slang for living easily and/or luxuriously. As Irish as Paddy's pig is quintessential Irishness.

To make a pig of oneself is self-explanatory. More modern is to pig out, as with most phrases ending in "out" (e.g., drop out, tune out, opt out).

Pig-headed, like bull-headed, is stubborn but also means less yielding to humans (no one says horse-headed …).

Pig-ignorant is extremely dumb, ignorant or crude. Pig iron is crude iron, initially from a smelting furnace in the form of oblong blocks.

An early mention of pig Latin, a non-Latin sort of juvenile code language, occurred in *Putnam's* magazine in 1869, but it was popularized via Hollywood golden-era movies. The ig-pay atin-Lay "code" is easily cracked.

A pignut, from the parsley family, is an earthnut and is also called a hognut (see the previous Hog section).

Pigskin is a US name for a football. A pigpen or pigsty may be certain children's bedrooms.

Pigtails are plaited locks of hair worn singly on the back or on each side of a girl's head. A pigtail is also a twist of tobacco or a short length of braided wire joining a stationary part of an electrical device to a moving part.

Pigweed is a North American plant used for fodder but a weed in most other countries.

Pigsticking was the so-called sport of hunting wild boar on horseback, using a spear.

A guinea pig is a tailless South American cavy or rodent, now fully domesticated and used as a pet or lab animal. A person may be a guinea pig, wittingly or not.

A bandicoot is a mostly insectivorous marsupial found in Australia and New Guinea whose name originated in the 1700s from a Telugu word meaning pig-rat.

Pork...

Pork is from Latin *porcus*, meaning pig, so Porky Pig's name is like saying Piggy Pig. (Which is fun to say.)

To pork out is to pig out. A porker is a young pig fattened for the kill or a fat person. A porkling is a small or young pig, not yet doomed to be a porker.

Pork pie is a British raised pie with minced cooked pork in it, eaten cold. A pork-pie hat has a flat crown and a brim that's turned up all around.

Porky is US slang for a porcupine, while pork barrel is an American term coined in the early 20th century from a barrel that held a reserve of meat—it means the corrupt practice of using government funds for projects that win votes.

FYI, the "decorative" apple in a roast pig's mouth is inserted afterward, else the poor dead porker would be drooling applesauce.

Pig Ears

A pig's ear is reportedly the sole part of that animal which cannot be eaten or somehow used. Ergo, in the Middle Ages when a craftsman's apprentice tried but failed to produce something useful or made a muddle of an assignment, he was said to have made a pig's ear.

In a pig's ear is a now obsolete alternative for in a pig's eye, which also expresses disbelief.

Pig's ear is Cockney rhyming slang for beer.

You can't make a silk purse out of a sow's ear is common sense about not being able to make a quality item out of inferior material. This was an established expression by the 16th century. In 1579 *The Ephemerides of Phialo* noted, "Seeking too (sic) make a silke purse of a Sowes eare, that when it shoulde close, will not come togeather." Some say it's a sow's ear instead of a male pig's because purse is a feminine item; however, purse back then didn't have the feminine connotation it does today.

Piggy Bank, Piggyback

Why a piggy bank and not a doggy bank or a kitty bank? (In fact one does "feed the kitty.") Because "piggy" evolved from pygg, the name of a clay once widely used in Britain to make kitchen earthenware items. People often used to store money in kitchen jars and pots made of pygg, ergo pygg jars, later pig jars, later pig banks. Eventually, for humor's sake, pig banks were molded in the shape of pigs.

After adults became comfortable with putting their money in real banks, the former pygg jars were used for spare change and often called penny banks. When they became popular for teaching children thrift and saving, they were renamed piggy banks.

In parts of Britain, pigs or china pigs are clay bottles used as bed warmers, sometimes in the shape of pigs.

Regarding "piggyback," precious few pigs would allow themselves to be carried that way. Again, the term originally had aught to do with animals. In the 1500s "pick pack" or "pick back" was a way of carrying something on one's back that by the 1700s had changed to "pick a pack," which was too close to "piggyback" to resist. Though now usually associated with a child carried on an adult's back, piggyback also denotes one thing stacked atop another, like trucks on flatbed railway cars.

Piggy...

"This little piggy went to market" begins the famous 18th-century nursery rhyme in which very young toes represent five little piggies, one of whom eats roast beef and one of whom, by inclination or lack, has none.

The adjective piggy can refer to a person's appetite or facial features. Crooner Dick Haymes, once as popular as Frank Sinatra, was noted for his porcine nose; he was nonetheless good-looking (one wife was "love goddess" Rita Hayworth).

Piggy in the Middle is a British game wherein two players try to throw a ball to each other without the person in between catching it. The expression also indicates somebody put in an awkward situation between two other people.

On little and big screens, the Muppets often spotlighted Miss Piggy, whose point, besides bedeviling Kermit the Frog, seemed to be female assertiveness and pride in, well, porkiness.

Male Chauvinist Pig

This 1970s term for the opposite of a feminist borrowed "pig" from the '60s American slang reference to policemen as porky, fat, and animalistic. Chauvinism is one of many French words extracted from the surnames of real people, including silhouette, mesmerism, and guillotine. Nicolas Chauvin was a French general under Napoleon noted for his excessive patriotism— that is, at the expense of other countries. Often abbreviated MCP, the term for someone with no respect for women as individuals may or may not have been coined by a female.

Piggle...

The verb "to piggle" is found in relatively few dictionaries. It has or had various meanings, most of dubious origin. The obvious one is to scarf down food ... like a pig. It's also to root for potatoes by hand. In England's East Midlands dialect it meant to pick at a scab. The noun piggle was a multi-pronged hook for rooting potatoes or mixing materials like clay and mortar together (mixing with a hook?). Today a piggle is a cross between a pit bull and a beagle—talk about an identity crisis.

In 1947 author Betty MacDonald launched the beloved Mrs. Piggle-Wiggle children's series. She'd already published *The Egg and I*, which became a hit movie and spawned the Ma and Pa Kettle film series. Post-*All in the Family*, Jean Stapleton played Mrs. Piggle-Wiggle, who cleverly and whimsically teaches children with bad habits to reform.

Higgledy-piggledy is too seldom heard—or read—these days. An adverb and adjective, it means in disorder—like helter-skelter, minus its negative connotation. Originating in the late 1500s, the childlike rhyming phrase may have referred to the erratic herding together of pigs.

Rabbit Mascots

One of the longest-lasting animal mascots is B'rer Rabbit (originally Brother Rabbit), jauntily featured on containers of Brer Rabbit Molasses. The likeable trickster, not unlike Bugs Bunny, had his own comic strip, "Uncle Remus and His Tales of B'rer Rabbit" from 1945 to 1972.

Another long-eared icon was the Bosco Rabbit. The chocolate syrup, which kids mixed into milk, was extremely popular in the 1950s and '60s. It came in a bunny-shaped plastic container; today the product is only regional. The Quik Bunny, with great floppy ears, was used to sell Nestle's Quik, a powder—also available in strawberry—mixed into milk.

From its second issue on, *Playboy* magazine has featured a rabbit on its cover, though it wasn't the original choice. Hugh Hefner was going to name his magazine *Stag Party*, until *Stag* magazine threatened to sue.

One of the most entertaining mascots is the Trix Rabbit, introduced in 1959. Described as a lovable loser, he knows what he wants—a bowl of Trix cereal—but never gets it because "Silly rabbit, Trix are for kids." Psychoanalysts have attributed the character's great success to children identifying with TR, since they too often don't get what they want.

The Energizer Bunny who goes on and on and on has sold countless batteries in a lengthy parade of award-winning commercials, eventually costarring in ads with Dracula, King Kong, Wile E. Coyote, and Darth Vader.

Welsh Rabbit

In 1725, according to the *Standard Oxford English Dictionary*, the dish comprising melted cheese and butter mixed with seasoning and poured over buttered toast was called Welsh rabbit. By 1785 it was Welsh rarebit. Why? Etymologizing, whereby a word that makes no sense—what rabbit?—is changed to one that does or makes more sense (even if none of those ingredients is rare).

It's not known why it was originally called Welsh rabbit. But then, mock-turtle soup has no turtle in it (it's made from calf's head, no comment) and Bombay duck is a fish. Aren't people funny, though?

Rabbits and Hares

In North America, rabbit means a rabbit or a hare. The latter, usually larger, has very long hind legs and is renowned for speed. In Britain, to hare is to run very fast.

To run with the hare and hunt with the hounds means to keep on good terms with both sides in a conflict; thus a secondary meaning is to be insincere or opportunistic.

To chase every hare is to be easily sidetracked.

Mad as a March hare vies with mad as a hatter in *Alice in Wonderland* in terms of erratic behavior. March is the rutting season during which hares supposedly go mad, leaping, boxing, and chasing over the countryside. To fly like a March hare combines the animal's swiftness and the intensity of that particular month.

First catch your hare is a mostly British expression saying to do things in an orderly and prepared manner. It's from the recipe on how to cook a hare from the celebrated *Mrs. Beeton's Cook Book*, published in 1861.

A harelip, also known as a cleft lip, is named after the perceived resemblance to a hare's mouth.

Bunny, a child's name for a rabbit, comes from 17th-century English dialect bun, a rabbit or squirrel. Bunny, rabbit, and hare all share an unfortunate reputation for fear and stupidity, reflected in such phrases as a dumb bunny, like a scared rabbit, and hare-brained (the latter also means rash—ill judgment born of speed). In Australia a bunny is also a human victim or a dupe. One factor in assuming rabbits are nervous or scared is their frequent but not constant nose twitching, which aids in their breathing and personal climate control.

In Britain, to "rabbit" is to chat informally, while "Rabbit, rabbit!" is a sexist phrase emulating talking women.

A "rabbit punch" is a swift chop applied to the back of someone's neck with the edge of the hand.

Rabbitfish have blunt noses and rabbit-like teeth or jaws. The Atlantic variety has the intriguing name *Chimaera monstrosa*.

To pull a rabbit out of a hat is a signature magic trick dating back to 1814 when Louis Comte—Count in English—was reportedly the first magician to do so. The expression signifies to effect or pull off a totally unexpected yet desirable solution.

Did you know "the rabbit test" required virgin female rabbits? Fortunately, animals are no longer used in pregnancy tests.

Pot Shot

A cooking pot whose primary ingredients were vegetable was typically always on the fire during the Middle Ages. (If the family could afford to spare a meal for a visitor, she or he was said to be given pot luck.) As for pot shot, it meant the hunter would shoot whatever animal crossed his path rather than track a specific game. Whatever he shot went into the family cooking pot.

The modern word meat is from Olde English mete, food or food item, of Germanic origin. Though once central to the language and to eating (meat used to mean the principal meal), today meat has several negative connotations; some examples: meathead or meatball—both dumbbells—or meat market—a place for sexual pickups—meat—a person as sexual object—or easy meat—somebody easily won over or outsmarted.

Porcupine and Hedgehog

The prickly porcupine got its name from the pig—animals were often named after others they resembled or barely resembled or not at all (a star*fish*?). "Porcupine" equals Latin *porcus spina*—thorn pig. Those familiar with porcupines (hopefully not with their quills) nickname them porkies. Further removed is the spiny porcupine fish that inflates itself when threatened.

Hedgehog pudding isn't what it sounds like (neither is carrot cake). The name of this nocturnal, insectivorous mammal that hardly resembles a hog and bears spines is used in the names of fruits and plants with spines, for instance, the hedgehog cactus. Hedgehog pudding is a variation on England's tipsy cake, soaked in alcohol and engulfed in custard or syllabub—sweetened milk or cream, slightly curdled with wine. Unlike the cake, the pudding is decorated with slivered almonds sticking out like spines.

A famous fairy tale is "Hans, My Hedgehog," about a half-human, half-hedgehog boy who evolves into a full human. A once nationally recognized mascot was Poppy the porcupine, who for a while replaced Sugar Pops Pete (who had a western image, less popular in the 1960s). Today the cereal is called Corn Pops—it sounds healthier, anyway.

Kidnapping

By any name, kidnapping—usually with ransom money as its goal—has existed for millennia (because of their wealth, royalty and nobility were the usual targets). One American explanation for the word is that since 1893 the US Navy's mascot has been a goat ... a kid named El Cid (after the medieval Spanish hero) was once stolen by cadets as a prank.

"Kidnapper" was first recorded in 1678 and originated as criminal slang (kid didn't always mean solely a goat or a child). Napper was already an established term for a thief, from the verb to nap or steal—related to the still-current to nab (to seize something or catch someone). When first described in print, kidnappers were men who illegally and by force secured laborers to toil in plantations in British colonies in North America and elsewhere.

The verb to kidnap was first recorded four years later, in 1682, likely as a back-formation, on the logical assumption that what kidnappers do is kidnap. The subsequent broader definition of kidnapping—beyond shanghaiing laborers— came later. As did Robert Louis Stevenson's seagoing novel *Kidnapped*, in 1886.

Getting Someone's Goat

Because goats were long thought to have a calming effect on horses, they were sometimes stabled with high-strung race horses, especially at an unfamiliar race track. Trying to crush a competing favorite's chances of winning was easier than today; a traditional ploy was sneaking into a targeted stable to steal the goat away. When the horse's owner found out somebody had gotten his goat, he was furious. (Today, some- one whose goat is gotten is more likely to be frustrated or upset—unless a race or money is involved.)

Some say the phrase didn't originate with horse racing. One alternative is the French phrase *prendre la chevre*, to take the goat, meaning to take a person's final resource (e.g., someone who's left with just a goat after losing a more valu- able cow, horse or pig). Others claim the phrase derives from goatee, a pointy chin beard resembling a billy goat's, often called a "goat" in the 1800s. Pulling, or getting, the goat could obviously irritate its owner.

An early written example occurs in a 1910 letter from Jack London: "Honestly, I believe I've got Samuels' goat! He's afraid to come back." That usage reveals fear. Currently, the phrase evinces anger, as in "That really gets my goat."

Scapegoat

This ancient concept dates back to the ancient Hebrews. It was Moses who decided that for the Day of Atonement (Yom Kippur) two goats should be led to the tabernacle's altar where the high priest would draw lots: one goat for God, one for Azazel, a desert demon. The first goat would be sacrificed. The second would, by confession, be symbolically laden with the people's sins of the past year and sent into the wilderness, carrying said sins away. Ironic that the demon's goat was the one that had a chance of survival. Cruelly ironic that in the Common Era Jews were often made scapegoats by Christians and, more recently, Muslims.

Horn of Plenty

In Greek mythology Zeus was suckled as an infant by a goat nymph named Amalthea (meaning tender). When he became the chief god, Zeus honored Amalthea by placing her image among the stars as Capricorn (the Goat). He also borrowed one of her sizeable horns and made it into a cornucopia, a horn of plenty that was perpetually full with food and drink for its owners. Cornucopias have long been a symbol—and decoration—associated with Thanksgiving.

Pan was a Greek demigod, patron of herds and flocks, forests and wildlife. He often played the Pan-pipes and was half-man, half-goat. When people heard his eerie music they were sometimes overcome by a sudden fear and confusion called panic.

Goat...

Interestingly, goat in Britain is slang for a dullard or stupid person, in the US for a lecherous man—and an old goat presumably for a dirty old man. Why the goat was chosen from all barnyard animals to represent lechery or stupidity isn't clear. Some sources say lechery because the male exudes a primitive musky odor. Some say stupidity because of the caprine habit of mindless butting, others because goats will eat anything, including tin cans (isn't that called recycling?).

Goat is also used for one who takes the blame (see Scapegoat), as in "Don't make me the goat!"

A goat-antelope is a naturally occurring ruminant that combines characteristics of goats and antelopes. Goatfish is a North American name for red mullet, and a goat moth is so-called because its caterpillar gives off a goatlike smell!

Goatsucker is another name for nightjar, a nocturnal insectivorous bird with a call that reminds some people of a goat's bleat. (A go-away bird is a long-tailed African bird whose call purportedly sounds like the words "go away.") And goat's beard is a dandelion-like plant with slender grasslike leaves that resemble, what else, a billy goat's beard or … goatee.

The End of One's Tether

In the Middle Ages—aren't you glad we live in the age of anesthesia?—grazing animals such as goats were frequently tethered to a post, keeping them within a restricted area. An animal was usually content so long as it could graze, but once it grazed up to the end of its tether and couldn't access greener pastures, frustration, anger, and despair set in. Also known as reaching the end of one's rope.

Sheep and Lambs

It doesn't take much ovine observation to see why people called sheep are easily led or influenced. Sheep are among the least resistant, most flock-oriented animals. Yet sheepish, applied to a human, means embarrassed from shyness or shame, and making sheep's eyes at somebody is amorous in a foolish way that doesn't necessarily entail embarrassment.

There are black sheep in every flock is the 19th-century expression that birthed the phrase black sheep of the family.

It arose from prejudice against the color black and standing out, and indicated that there are miscreants in every family, group, community, and congregation (ovine references are religious staples).

Prior to the 1830s English punishments for crimes were unduly harsh, resulting in the expression may as well be hanged for a sheep as a lamb. Stealing a sheep incurred the death penalty, as did stealing various smaller animals, including a lamb. So a thief reckoned he might as well steal the larger animal and get more meat, as it entailed the same risk. A more modern expression meaning the same thing is in for a penny, in for a pound—that is, may as well go all the way.

Why do people count sheep to (try to) fall asleep? Because ovine flocks are typically the biggest, with the most individual members to count.

A flock of sheep, if human, is a bunch of go-along-ers.

A biblical saying is to separate the sheep from the goats, representing separating good people from bad people, reflecting the anti-goat bias of ancient times (see Scapegoat).

Condoms used to be known as sheepskins because they were made from the intestinal membrane of a lamb.

To wait two shakes of a lamb's tail is to wait a very short while.

Meek as a lamb speaks for itself. A sacrificial lamb is someone unfairly made to pay for others' mistakes or misdeeds. To go like a lamb to the slaughter connotes somebody facing their destruction docilely—the difference being that animals don't know what awaits them.

Wool...

Dyed in the wool, a trade term used in English wool mills, was first recorded in 1579. Wool dyed before being treated retained its color far better than wool dyed after weaving (known as dyed in the piece). Eventually dyed in the wool stood for anything or anyone not easily altered by another process—including persuasion; the phrase is frequently used in a political context.

Speaking of sheep's clothing, the sneaky wolf in it goes way back, including Aesop's fables and the Bible.

Fleece, what sheep wear, got twisted into a verb meaning to monetarily overcharge someone. The implication was that if you were overcharged enough, it was like a sheep losing its fleece—or a person losing their shirt.

Wool-gathering is indulgence in idle or aimless thought, such as a shepherd might do.

Woolly can mean confused or vague, as in woolly thinking. Agatha Christie described her elderly sleuth Miss Marple as seeming woolly via her soft white hair and an absentminded air that masked detecting talents which outdid the police.

A woolly bear is no cuddly teddy bear, but a big hairy caterpillar, particularly that of a tiger moth. It's also the small hairy larva of a carpet beetle or museum beetle.

Wool-sorters' disease is a form of anthrax in humans that causes pneumonia. (Anthrax is an ovine and bovine bacterial disease that affects the lungs and skin and can be transmitted to humans.)

And Woolloomooloo is a suburb of Sydney, Australia.

Bigwig

Bigwig, for an important person, is now a less popular term than, say, a big cheese, the big enchilada, or the head honcho. However, the older term was literal, as an individual's status was often conflated with the size of their wig—who had bigger ones than Louis XVI and Marie Antoinette before they lost their heads? Wigs were made of various materials, including wool, horse hair, and human hair. In France and England, thieves (who'd sometimes resorted to theft only to avoid starvation, hence the eventual French Revolution) often drew near their rich victims from behind, then pulled the big wig down and forward over the aristocrat's eyes to distract them and gain time while robbing them. In more democratic times, the phrase to pull the wool over someone's eyes merely indicates fooling or deceiving them.

Mutton, Chops

Mutton is the mature flesh of sheep, as food. The phrase mutton dressed up as lamb derides an older woman dressed like a younger one. A man's mutton chop whiskers resemble a meat chop, narrow at the top and wide and rounded below.

Muttonhead is an old word for a stupid or dull person. Its abbreviation, mutt, eventually acquired a canine application.

A mutton bird is a long-winged seabird so named because its cooked flesh recalls the taste of mutton (not chicken).

Chops are a human's or animal's mouth, jaws, or cheeks. They're also what one licks in anticipation of or after eating something delicious. Chops is related to the 16th-century chap, the lower jaw or half of the cheek, particularly of a pig when used for food.

Chops are also the technical skill of a rock or jazz musician.

To bust one's chops is to put forth extra effort. To bust someone else's chops is to nag or criticize them.

Rats

"I smell a rat." This phrase denoting suspicion without concrete evidence is due to the fact that a human may not be able to smell a rat, but a dog with its far keener sense of smell can. In not so merry olde England rats were a major problem. When a dog unexpectedly began sniffing around a house or barn, its owner was wont to say that it looked like the dog smelled a rat. The proof usually came later.

Calling someone a rat has been an international pejorative for millennia, rats being among the most despised and feared of animals for health, economic, and aesthetic reasons.

Gangster-film star James Cagney made a 1930s catchphrase of you dirty rat, often referring to an informer (or stool pigeon). Prison slang had already made rat, dirty rat, rat fink—also cornered like a rat—common in-house terms.

Apart from ratty, rat can prefix or be added to most anything dirty or unpleasant, like a rathole or the rat race. In Britain a ratbag is somebody unpleasant or disliked, and rat-arsed (-assed, in the US) means very drunk.

A rat pack is a group of aggressive associates or close-knit friends. The original Hollywood rat pack comprised Humphrey Bogart and his drinking buddies, including Frank Sinatra, who later wanted to marry Bogart's widow, Lauren Bacall. In the US rat can specify someone associated with a given place, such as a mall rat or gym rat.

Ratlines are a series of small rope lines attached to a sailing ship's shrouds (the rigging ropes that help support the mast or topmast) like ladder rungs, for rigging or climbing.

A rat snake is a harmless—to humans—constrictor that squeezes and eats rats and other small mammals. A rat-kangaroo is a small Australian marsupial that resembles a rat, has long hind legs, and hops.

A hair rat or hair bun rat is indirectly familiar to anyone who's seen 1940s movies. Going back centuries, these sausage-shaped coiffeur-shapers were often ten inches long. A brunette one allegedly resembled a rat. A woman's hair was wound over the flexible rat, yielding the puffy yet sculpted hairstyles that were especially popular during the Victorian era and the '40s.

"Drat!"—a pet exclamation of W. C. Fields—does not, as urban legend has it, stand for damn rat, but is a 19th-century contraction of God rot, highly blasphemous at the time.

Topo Gigio

Arguably the most popular guest on TV's long-running and star-studded *The Ed Sullivan Show* was Topo Gigio, the Italian mouse who appeared some 50 times between 1963 and '71 when the variety series ended. Sullivan believed that his banter with the adorable mouse—*topo*; Gigio is a nickname for Luigi/Louis—warmed his semifrozen image. Gigio clearly had a crush on Sullivan, bashfully flirting with him, eventually cooing "I love you, Eddie," and wangling a kiss.

Ten inches tall with doe-like eyes cut from foam rubber, Topo Gigio could talk, walk, roll his eyes, wiggle his ears and toes, and gesture—all at the same time. He was created by Maria Perego Caldura of Milan, who performed all his movements except for his hands and arms, which two other also unseen puppeteers controlled while a fourth individual supplied the cuddly rodent's voice.

Before Sullivan, Gigio made an Italian movie (later released in the US as *The Magic World of Topo Gigio*). During Sullivan he was marketed as toys and trinkets, afterward appearing in cartoons, doing world tours—he was a smash in Japan—and starring in his own children's TV show in Italy, where he still performs at festivals.

Build a Better Mousetrap

Back in the day, mousetraps were far more important than they are now. This expression about making a major improvement to a product (or method) likely originated with Ralph Waldo Emerson. The essayist-poet-philosopher-lecturer was a leader of the Hindu-inspired American Transcendentalist movement, which purposed personal transcendence and the philosophy God-is-everywhere-including-within-you.

Self-publicizing writer Elbert Hubbard, renowned in the early 20th century for his "pithy sayings," claimed the mousetrap phrase as his own. Eventually he was contradicted by Sarah Yule, whose 1889 anthology *Borrowings* quoted Emerson: "If a man can write a better book, preach a better sermon, or make a better mousetrap than his neighbor, though he build his house in the woods, the world will make a beaten path to his door."

Yule declared she'd jotted down the quote during an Emerson lecture in 1871.

Today the phrase is invariably used in a business context, and has been shortened to: "Build a better mousetrap and the world will beat a path to your door."

Bats and Batty

Interesting that mental illness only afflicts humans, yet some animals are considered crazier than others. Sometimes on account of a habit like sleeping upside down and only coming out at night. Isn't that batty? So a crazy or nutty person is deemed batty. The term was reinforced by a famous and controversial book, *Treatise on Madness*, that well predated Freud, by one William Battie (1704–1776), a psychiatrist. And by the famous case of a barrister from Spanish Town, Jamaica, later certified insane in London in 1839, named Fitzherbert Batty.

Bats sound asleep in a belfry—a bell tower or steeple—when bells are suddenly loudly rung tend to become madly agitated (who wouldn't?).

Interesting too that in the centuries before books became widely and cheaply available, slang expressions that were commonly spoken didn't necessarily find their way into print. For instance the word batty doesn't appear to have seen print until about 1900.

Like a Bat Out of Hell

Among mammals, only bats can fly. (In German bat is *Fledermaus*, incorporating the word for mouse.) Some

2,400 years ago, Aristophanes mentioned a bat from hell in his play *The Birds*. Because they sleep in dark caves and spaces by day and swoop out at night, often startlingly fast, bats have long been associated with "hell" or the underworld.

The discovery and subsequent publicity attending the vampire bat, found in many tropic regions, especially Latin America, added to bats' hellish reputation. Vampire bats suck and subsist on blood after piercing a victim with razor-like incisors (while sucking, they pee, to render their bodies light enough to fly). Dracula and Batman—and to a lesser extent plays like *The Bat* and operas like *Die Fledermaus*—have given this unique creature a permanently extended lease on cultural life.

Speed was the point of this expression. For example in George Patullo's 1912 novel *The Sheriff of Badger*: "Whenever I have any (money) and get to town, it goes like a bat out of hell." As the 1900s wore on, the expression acquired a connotation of speed driven by fear—as opposed to, say, spending money quickly.

Bat Conservation International reports that one species of bat flies as fast as 60 miles per hour. All bats are equipped with echolocation, which enables them to fly unhesitantly through complete darkness. Neat, huh?

(Though bats can sleep and hibernate upside down, to give birth or go to the bathroom they must hang by their thumbs right-side-up.)

Badger...

Dachshund means badger dog in German, for so-called wiener dogs were specifically bred, via their distinctive shape,
to dig badgers out of their setts or burrows. Members of the
weasel family, badgers are nocturnal omnivores, usually black
and gray with a white-striped head.

The cruel pastime of badger-baiting, illegal in the UK
since 1830, involved dogs luring a badger from its sett and
ripping it to pieces.

Bald as a badger doesn't make sense—they don't look
bald, unlike a coot—until one completes the original phrase:
bald as a badger's bum (UK bum is US buttocks or buns).
Not that a badger's bum looks bald either, but it was once
widely believed that shaving-brush bristles were plucked
from that particular venue.

As for how that unobtrusive animal became associated
with the verb to badger or repeatedly nag or bother someone,
that involved another "sport," in which dogs were unleashed
upon a badger that had been put in an upturned barrel. After
dragging it out, a non-humane human placed the bloodied
badger back in the barrel so the dogs could drag it out again,
and again if need be, until it was an unrecognizable pulp.

Weasel and Ferret

The weasel, a small, slender carnivore related to stoats, ferrets,
and minks, has an undeservedly nasty reputation. A human

weasel is cunning and treacherous, weaseling his way out of deceitful situations of his own making.

Weasel words are either misleading or ambiguous or they're words or phrases that weaken the meaning of those preceding them, the premise being that they suck the life out of those words the way a weasel sucks eggs out of their shells. Example: "I promise to be faithful, honey, as long as I find you attractive." Or: "I love you in that dress, I don't care what anyone says."

A ferret is a domesticated weasel-like mammal employed to enter burrows and chase rabbits out of their warrens, into the near presence of humans with shotguns. (The practice is alas illegal only in some places.) Ergo the expression to ferret something out—to search for or investigate something thoroughly.

Pop Goes the Weasel

This supposed children's ditty that was once a dance goes back centuries and is today mainly associated with musical jack-in-the-boxes. Everybody knows the tune, almost nobody knows the lyrics. Over time, it's had a variety of lyrics, sometimes with one animal chasing another or an animal chasing a man, but inevitably ending with pop goes the weasel. (Wind-up musical boxes feature a pop-up clown rather than a weasel, which unless accurately reproduced might resemble a rat and scare children.) English writer Quentin Crisp, who penned a foreword for one of this author's books, recalled "the most popular version" that he knew as a child:

Up and down the City Road/In and out the Eagle/ That's the way the Money goes/Pop goes the Weasel.

It featured, Crisp explained, Cockney rhyming slang. The City Road was a London street and the Eagle a real pub. Pop was slang for to pawn something and weasel for a tailor's iron. Translation: a tailor must pawn his means of livelihood because he's spent all his money at his favorite pub. Kids' stuff?

Playing Possum

A set of related animal expressions often dwindle with time to just one, as with the 19th century's to act possum, to come possum over someone, to play possum (the survivor), and the verb—as in "With my eyes closed I possumed sleep."

An opossum or possum is a marsupial with a prehensile tail and hind feet with an opposable thumb that routinely plays dead when attacked, sometimes lying still for hours and fooling its attacker, who moves on. One of the earliest examples of a human mimicking the marsupial is found in William Ioor's 1807 *The Battle of Eutaw Springs and*

Evacuation of Charleston: "They little thought I was playing 'possum' all the while! ... Now, if I could only stumble upon proof positive that I was the first clever fellow who saved his life by dying."

The phrase's meanings of feigning death or sickness or sleep have by now mostly dwindled to the latter.

P.S. An opossum shrimp isn't even a shrimp, but a separate crustacean. The opossum part of the name comes from its pouch, in which eggs and young are carried.

Big Bad Wolves

In English, the wolf has a bad reputation, and not just because of the Three Little Pigs. He—we usually assume it's a he, unless it's a she-wolf, like the one that gave suck to Romulus and Remus—is a deceiver, as with Little Red Riding Hood, as a wolf in sheep's clothing (Aesop again), and he's sometimes a lech, a sex-minded wolf who emits wolf whistles. Or he's a rapacious collector or scammer—a wolf at the door. Sometimes he's a nasty hybrid: a werewolf.

British zoologist Dr. Gil Ferguson adds, "The wolf is the largest member of the dog family. Its appearance may fool us into thinking 'dog,' but its behavior is often not human-friendly. Which can induce a feeling of betrayal. Besides, where a dog is happy to bond with a human and virtually forsake other canines, the wolf is very much a pack animal, therefore more aloof to us and far more intimidating."

A lone wolf is a very independent human who prefers minimal contact with his own kind. In this regard, a dog is more of a "lone wolf" than a wolf is.

Unless one actually sees a big bad wolf, one should never cry wolf (thank you, Aesop).

To wolf something down is to eat ravenously, hardly chewing, like a hungry wolf.

To throw or feed someone to the wolves is to sacrifice a friend or other non-stranger in order to avoid trouble or save one's own skin (or hide), also to make somebody else a scapegoat for one's own sake or safety.

Other Wolves

Whereas in English the only semipositive way to label a man a wolf is via the womanizer reference, wolves come off better in some other languages. In French, *mon loup*, my wolf, is an endearment, usually man to man, as in traditional English's old chap or old bean. The womanizer-as-wolf equivalent in Italian uses an entirely different animal: *pappagallo*, parrot! However, in Europe a wolf or other whistle has usually signified disapproval, not admiration or lust.

Ironically, a wolfhound is a large dog breed originally used for hunting wolves.

The sizeable wolf fish, also called a sea wolf, has a long body, long dorsal fin, and sharp teeth. (In some cultures the shark is known as the wolf of the sea.)

A wolf spider is a fast-moving ground spider known for running after and jumping on its prey (not all spiders spin webs).

A wolverine, despite its name deriving from wolf, isn't one, though it's heavily built (but short-legged) and carnivorous.

Wolfram's not an animal, but tungsten or its ore, the name from wolf and *ram*, a Germanic word meaning soot that refers to miners having deprecated tungsten ore as inferior to tin.

Fox...

The expression "sour grapes" is so universal it's often forgotten that its source was an Aesop fable called "The Fox and the Grapes," wherein a fox exerts much effort in trying to grab a bunch of grapes high on a vine. In vain. Thereafter he explains that he stopped trying, really didn't want them, because they looked sour.

"Crazy like a fox" is a misnomer. Obviously they're not, and don't even give the impression—unlike squirrels, which aren't either. The original uncorrupted expression was "cunning like a fox." Foxes have a canny reputation ("can" originally meant to know, related to the word ken). In a 1980 interview, Judy Carne said of her former *Rowan & Martin's Laugh-In* costar Goldie Hawn, "She's not a dizzy blonde. She's about as dumb as a fox."

The foxtrot was reportedly named after American comedian Harry Fox, whose 1913 *Ziegfeld Follies* turn included its steps. The dance's rhythm alternates fast and slow steps that some have likened to certain aspects of horsemanship. Foxtrot is also radio communication's code word for the letter F.

A fox is a sexy female and foxy means sexy, while to fox someone is to deceive or baffle them, but foxed also denotes the brownish spots on discolored paper in old books and prints.

A foxhole is a space too limited for one's needs or comfort and was a hole in the ground used by military troops, especially during World War I.

Foxfire is phosphorescent light emitted by particular fungi in a decaying wood.

Foxglove is a tall plant with pink-purple flowers shaped like the fingers of a glove, also known as digitalis and a poison familiar to readers of Agatha Christie.

Foxtail is meadow grass with soft, bushy flowering spikes.

A foxhound, smooth-coated with droopy ears, was bred to hunt foxes in packs. A fox terrier—a short- or wire-haired breed—was originally used to unearth foxes.

Camel Cigarettes and a Straw

A dromedary known as Old Joe has adorned Camel cigarette packs since 1913. The original model performed for the Barnum & Bailey circus. When B&B arrived in the Winston-Salem area, the R.J. Reynolds company requested to photograph the creature. The circus refused until the tobacco company hinted that few people might visit the circus at night if their ciga-rette plant stayed open. However, Old Joe wouldn't stand still for the shot, so the handler slapped his face. Old Joe raised his tail and drew back his ears, a drom-edary's way of expressing anger. That was the picture the tobacco people chose to use.

The younger, hipper, anthropomorphic Joe Camel debuted in the US in 1988 but had already been employed in France since 1974. Criticism was immediate. The American Cancer Society asked the Federal Trade Commission to ban Joe from ads, and many people charged that his face deliberately resembled a penis, which the illustrator and the ad company denied.

In 1655 Archbishop John Bramhall wrote, "It is the last feather that breaks the horse's back." A later varia-tion substituted straw and a camel and was made popu-lar by Charles Dickens in his 1848 novel *Dombey and Son*: "As the last straw breaks the laden camel's back ...."

FYI, a dromedary camel can drink 30 gallons of water in 10 minutes. (And they say "drinks like a fish.")

Kangaroo Court

A "kangaroo court" is an irregular, illegal, and/or mock tribu-nal or court of justice. In 19th-century America, particularly in the Old West and the South, it was all too common for court procedure to skip steps or ethics in order to arrive at a quick, convenient, or popular verdict. This was called jumping through the procedure of justice, first recorded in 1853 and associated with the California gold rush of 1849 that drew prospectors from around the world, including a disproportionate number of Australians. Disputes raged between regular prospectors and illegal ones, often called claim jumpers. Alleged courts were set up to try-and-convict irregular prospectors, sometimes for no better reason than that they were Aussies or other foreigners; these became known as kangaroo courts.

The term later became well known in Britain via trade unions setting up tribunals to try members considered to be strike-breakers.

(Ever wondered if mother kangaroos clean their pouches? Of course they do. A joey may live in there up to eight months, thereafter going out for a walk or nosh but returning until joey's too big to fit or mama's had enough. She cleans joey's bedroom—it's also joey's bathroom; don't ask—by opening it with her forepaws, sticking her head in, and licking it spic and span. Nuff said.)

Freezing the Balls off a Brass Monkey

It must be pretty chilly if it's cold enough to freeze the balls off a brass monkey, but what does that expression signify? The gun powder required to fire the large guns on 18th-century man-of-war ships was stored in separate, confined areas for safety reasons. Small boys, typically orphans, were used to slip or crawl through small spaces and passageways to retrieve the powder. The boys were nicknamed monkeys, which in Britain often was and is applied to anyone mischievous, especially a child.

The brass trays which held the guns' cannonballs were called brass monkeys. Each tray had 16 cannonball-sized indentations that formed the base of a cannonball pyramid. The trays were made of brass because the cannonballs would stick to or rust on iron. However, brass contracts much quicker in cold weather than iron, so that on extremely cold days the indentations supporting the base level of cannonballs would contract, spilling the balls off the brass monkey. (Now you know.)

Monkey...

Not the best pets—they're definitely not domesticated—monkeys are nonetheless cute and amusing. What's more fun than a barrel of monkeys? Their image is irresponsibly playful—they love to monkey around (or horse around). They're reputed mischief-makers—though it's no fun having a monkey on your back—and quick to ape (!) others: monkey see, monkey do.

Interesting how despite education, so many people—the media is no corrective—routinely lump monkeys together with apes or call chimpanzees, humans' closest relatives, monkeys.

To make a monkey of someone is to ridicule or humiliate them, perhaps with the implication of lowering them a few rungs on the evolutionary ladder. I'll be a monkey's uncle—with possibly the same subconscious implication—indicates disbelief.

To not give a monkey's about something is UK slang for not caring at all (or giving a hoot). Cheeky monkey began as a Lancashire term for somebody with a lot of nerve. Monkey nut is a British name for a peanut.

Monkey wrench, a North American term for a spanner with an adjustable jaw, is said to have been invented by a London blacksmith named Charles Moncke or an American, circa 1856, named Mr. Monk.

To throw a monkey wrench into the works is to block its success. To monkey with means to interfere with or spoil. Monkey tricks (UK) or monkeyshines (US) implies mischievous behavior. Monkey business is mischievous or deceitful behavior.

A monkey jacket is a close-fitting short jacket worn by waiters, sailors, and officers in their mess. A monkey suit is a man's formal suit or tuxedo. Contrastingly, a grease monkey is a mechanic.

A monkey's fist is a knot that mariners use to help dock a ship.

A monkey engine is a piledriver with a heavy hammer or ram operating vertically in a groove.

Monkey bars are a playground staple, a horizontal over-head ladder for swinging along.

A monkey puzzle is a coniferous evergreen tree native to Chile with scaly branches (sounds more reptilian than simian), while a monkey flower is a plant of boggy ground whose red or yellow flowers resemble snapdragons. Obviously the common names of trees and plants—versus their Latin botanical names—weren't always chosen by scientific observers.

The original 17th-century carving representing the three monkeys that hear no evil, see no evil, and speak no evil is part of a shrine in Nikko, Japan. The simian legend was probably brought there in the 8th century, or Nara Period, by a Buddhist monk returning from China, where similar expressions were recorded in the 2nd to 4th centuries CE.

Ape

Apes don't have tails, as monkeys do, and are primates, which include chimpanzees, gorillas, orangutans, and gibbons. This is the closest animal group to homo sapiens, yet the word ape connotes physical and mental clumsiness, also aggression, as in you big ape or you dumb ape.

To go ape is to suddenly become angry or very excited. Apesh*t, American slang, means the same thing.

An apeman—but not Tarzan—is an extinct apelike primate thought to have been related to present-day humans.

Jackanapes is an archaic term for a tame monkey and a dated one for an uncouth or impertinent individual. (Jack was the most commonly used name in myriad expressions from jack o' lantern to jack-of-all-trades.)

To ape someone is to imitate them.

A goon may be a weird person or, more usually, a hired thug, and is sometimes said to be a cross between gorilla and baboon.

Bear...

Besides an ursine mammal, a bear can be a rough or ill-mannered human—"like a bear with a sore head" is a British expression for a very irritable person. Also, stock-market-wise (or unwise, as the case may be), a bear, contrasted with a bull, is somebody who sells shares in hope of repurchasing them later at a lower price. The phrase's origin is thought to be the proverb warning against "selling the bear's skin before one has caught the bear." A bear market is one in which share prices are falling.

Bear-baiting was long a popular form of entertainment—so were gladiatorial games—wherein dogs were loosed to attack a captive bear. A bear garden or bear pit denotes a scene of confusion and uproar, deriving from the 16th-century site set apart for bear-baiting.

A bear hug is one that's rough and really squeezes but is non-lethal from a human.

A bearing rein is a fixed rein that makes a horse raise its head and arch its back.

Bearskin is a tall cap of black fur worn ceremonially by various troops (often seen and photographed in London).

And there's the sloth bear, named after the animal that represents laziness. It lives on termites but has a major sweet tooth and will sometimes open a beehive and keep eating the honey after getting its nose stung several times.

(In case you ever wondered, when bears hibernate—spending winter in a dormant state—they don't eliminate their waste, but recycle it, converting the toxic compounds into protein. Researchers are studying this process in hopes of treating kidney failure in humans.)

Loaded for Bear

Once upon a time, North America abounded with black, Alaska brown, grizzly, and other bears. They were shot for food and "sport." Hunting bears required nerve and preparedness, and led to this expression, widespread by the 1880s. The *New York World* in 1888 chronicled, sports-wise, "Ewing was loaded for bear and was just spoiling for a chance to catch somebody on the bases." Two years later the *Dictionary of Slang, Jargon and Cant* advised, "Loaded for bears (sic) ... signifies that a man is slightly intoxicated, enough to feel ready to confront danger."

Today the phrase usually means to be very well prepared or aggressively hoping for a fight.

Bear Plants

Bear with me here. Bearberry is a creeping dwarf shrub with pink flowers and red berries, a member of the heather family. Beargrass is a North American plant with long thick leaves, including wild yucca. Bear's breech, a Mediterranean plant, has big leaves and tall spikes of purple-veined white flowers. Bear's ear is the nickname for auricula, an Alpine primula that supposedly resembles bear's ears. And bear's foot is the nickname for hellebore, a poisonous winter-flowering plant with big green, white, or purple flowers whose thick divided leaves supposedly resemble a bear's foot.

To Lick Something Into Shape

In the distant past, before science—sometimes seemingly before logic—some cultures believed that particular animals, especially bears, birthed formless babies that had to be licked into the shape of their breed. Of course many animals are born enveloped in thick afterbirth that makes them nearly unrecognizable until the mother cleans it off. But as relatively late as 150 CE Aulus Gellius wrote, "For he said that as the bear brought forth her young formless and misshapen, by licking gave it form and shape."

Bear Mascots

When companies employ bears as advertising mascots, they fall into one of two categories: real bears or teddy bears. Two that weren't teddies were the long-running brown bear which pitched Hamm's Beer and Teddy Snow Crop, the polar bear used to advertise Snow Crop Frozen Orange Juice. (Did you know polar bears have black skin but white fur, and that each hair is in fact a hollow tube which funnels sun rays to the bear's skin to keep it warm? Polar bears appear white because the rays bounce off their fur. Nature is amazing.)

Among teddy bears, Sugar Bear was the mascot for Post's Sugar Crisp cereal, singing, "Can't get enough Super Golden Crisp." After the sugar purge—of names, not ingredients—of the 1970s the product was renamed Super Golden Crisp. A charming little bear named Snuggles used to advertise Snuggles Fabric Softener, and for a long time TraveLodge motels featured Sleepy Bear, dressed in a nightcap and nightshirt, eyes half closed and arms outstretched, heading for bed. That very popular mascot successfully embodied two ursine aspects: teddy bears are used by children to help them sleep and bears are associated with comfortable hibernation.

Teddy bears were introduced in 1902 and named after President Theodore (Teddy) Roosevelt after he went on a hunting trip to Mississippi. The politician, who loved to hunt, went to shoot bears, but not many were left. Some batty locals tried to help by offering him a baby cub, but

Teddy preferred bigger game. Cartoonist Clifford Berryman drew an editorial cartoon of the episode, which gave Rose and Morris Mitchom of the Ideal Company the notion to manufacture little toy bears dressed like Roosevelt. Most teddy bears eventually went *au naturel.*

A koala is a marsupial, not a bear (nor is a panda), but the cognomen "koala bear" persists. One of the most famous advertising mascots of the late 20th century was the koala sitting in a tree bemoaning the impending surge of tourists to its native habitat due to Quantas' low airfares to Australia. "I hate Quantas," he grumbled. (Quantas stands for Queensland and Northern Territory Aerial Services.)

Though bears are large and often ferocious, as fictional characters they are beloved, for example, Paddington Bear, Winnie the Pooh, Baloo, Fozzie Bear, Yogi Bear (and Booboo too!). Likewise the most famous live bear, Smokey, the scourge of arsonists.

Squirrels

A squirrel is a cute tree-dwelling rodent with a bushy tail, famous for "squirreling" away nuts for later consumption and, partly due to its quick, seemingly erratic movements, for being "squirrely"—kooky or eccentric when applied to a human. The reason a squirrel moves its head from side to side before jumping is that it can't see straight ahead clearly; rather, its eyes allow it to see above, below and behind it without moving its head. The phrase nutty as a squirrel also reflects its penchant for nuts and seeds; however, squirrels are very methodical and well-adapted creatures.

Squirrel is used in the names of other members of the same family, for instance a ground squirrel.

A squirrel cage is a rotating cylindrical cage in which a small animal, like a hamster, can exercise on a treadmill. It's also a type of rotor in small electric motors that resembles a squirrel cage.

A squirrel monkey is a South American simian minus a prehensile tail that nonetheless leaps from tree to tree with the greatest of ease.

A squirrelfish is a brightly colored, big-eyed fish dwelling around reefs in warm seas. Its name reflects somebody's opinion that its eyes and the sound it makes resemble those of a squirrel.

Kellogg's created a character named Sugar Pops Pete to advertise its Sugar Pops cereal. Pete spoke with a whistle and used pistols to puff up the corn cereal with sugar, singing, "Oh, the pops are sweeter and the taste is new. They're shot with sugar, through and through." Pete was meant to be a ground squirrel, but the artist who drew him had no picture or photo for reference, so Pete was widely mistaken for a teddy bear! (Today the Pete-less cereal is named Corn Pops.)

Beaver...

Related to squirrels but bigger and amphibious, beavers are among the most intelligent and industrious of animals—hence, eager beavers. They build their own houses, canals, and dams up to about 1,500 feet in length. Propped on their hind legs, they can gnaw around and around a tree up to 18 inches or 46 centimeters in diameter until it falls. Beavers' prominent front teeth led to nicknaming some male children "Beaver," for example, Theodore Cleaver on TV's *Leave It to Beaver*. (A beaver is also a boy of six or seven affiliated with the Scout Association.)

Beavers alternate layers of mud, stone, and wood, cut by themselves, until a dam is tall enough. Dams enclose beavers' aquatic-vegetation food supply (water lilies, also wood, are favorite meals) and protect their communal house, known as a lodge, which has two underwater passages and doorways that lead to a main accommodation room and an area that's a larder or food store. Beavers are ever on the lookout for leaks, plugging up holes with mud and sticks. Most animals adapt to their environment, but beavers, like humans, considerably alter theirs.

Fortunately, beaver cloth merely resembles beaver fur and is a heavy woolen cloth. Beaver lamb is lambskin made to resemble beaver fur.

Beaver is also the lower part of the face guard of a helmet in a suit of armor (in *Hamlet*, Horatio says of the prince of Denmark's father's ghost, "… he wore his beaver up").

Beaver is an obsolete term for a bearded man. In the early 20th century children would sometimes call out, "Beaver!" when they spotted a man with a beard.

Beaverboard is any type of fiber board.

Due to a beaver's thick brown fur, beaver is slang for a well-haired pudendum, especially a woman's, and a beaver shot in pornography is a photograph of same. The 1984 US presidential election included the first-ever female candidate for vice-president, Geraldine Ferraro, and Walter Mondale. Opponents of the Democratic ticket printed bumper stickers referring to "Wally and the Beaver" (Wally Cleaver was Theodore's elder brother).

Among the best-known commercials of early television were those for Ipana toothpaste—formerly tooth powder— starring cute bucktoothed Bucky Beaver. In each ad, he would be confronted by D. K. Germ, a gray blob representing tooth decay, whom Bucky would fight by whipping out his tube of Ipana and knocking the big germ down. Despite the beaver's popularity and the prominence of Ipana, both are long gone.

I've Seen the Elephant

This ominous-sounding phrase was current in North America in the early and mid 1800s, particularly among settlers moving westward. The phrase could stand alone or be followed by: and I've heard the owl and I've been to the other side of the mountain. It asserted that the speaker wasn't a greenhorn, was somebody who'd been around, and had even faced danger. In those days, if you'd seen something as rare as an elephant, you'd seen plenty, brother (and sister too).

The word trunk was first used to describe a tree's main stem in the 1400s. The first use of trunk for an elephant's prehensile nose was in a 1565 translation by Richard Eden, whose specialty was books about geography, navigation, and travel.

White Elephant

In Siam, now Thailand, white elephants were rare and prized and automatically belonged to the king, as black swans still officially belong to the British monarch. White elephants were not to be worked or ridden, and so, though revered, were virtually useless. A royal custom developed whereby a subject who displeased the king was given a white elephant as a gift he could not refuse but had to care for. Such a "gift" could ruin someone financially. Siam was one of few Southeast Asian countries not conquered by the British or French, but the phrase was taken back to the UK in the mid 1700s and applied to expensive but useless buildings or monuments.

Of Mice and Memories

Contrary to myth, elephants are not afraid of mice. They fear only humans and—because they can kill baby elephants—lions and tigers. Elephants, who have poor eyesight, rely more on their sense of smell, and a mouse doesn't smell enough to concern an elephant. The myth began, like so many things, with the ancient Greeks, who spun a tale about a mouse that crawled up an elephant's trunk and drove the poor pachyderm insane. (Pachyderm means thick-skinned.)

An average elephant weighs between 5,000 and 14,000 pounds and consumes 300 to 500 pounds of vegetation daily. An elephant's trunk has over 40,000 muscles and is sensitive enough to pick up a rhinestone. Elephant brains, the largest of any land-based animal, are four times the size of a human brain.

It's been said that an elephant never forgets. But how much does an elephant have to remember? Elephants, like bulls, have been known to carry a grudge, and have longer memories than several mammals—they also live longer than most. According to Sri Lankan animal trainer Chana Bandaranaike, "Elephants are strong but sensitive, sometimes even delicate…. It is exciting and showman-like to exaggerate. But to say they never forget … even people forget."

Pachyderms

Elephantine describes elephants but also denotes largeness or, unfairly, clumsiness.

Elephantiasis is a grim Third World condition in which a limb, usually a leg, swells to elephant-like size due to vessel blockage by large parasitic worms.

A rogue elephant deserts the herd and conventional behavior, venting anger and destruction on all sides.

An elephant bird (*Aepyornis*) was a large flightless bird from Madagascar, now extinct.

An elephant seal is a large seal with an inflatable snout and very thick neck found on North America's west coast and around Antarctica.

An elephant shrew is a small insect-eating African mammal with a rat-like tail, long hind legs, and—thus, its name—a long mobile snout.

Elephant grass is very tall, hardy tropical African grass.

Pink elephants are what some people think they see during withdrawal (cold turkey or otherwise) from alcohol.

In 1960 General Mills introduced a cereal called Twinkles. To advertise it they chose an orange elephant named Twinkles, taken from a Saturday morning cartoon show called *King Leonardo and His Subjects*. Each cereal box had a small multi-page storybook about Twinkles built into its back panel. Kids loved the stories. More than the cereal. GM discontinued the cereal and the elephant.

(Sometimes kids ask, especially after attending the circus, can elephants jump? Basically, no. Because of their size and strength, elephants have no natural predators and don't need to jump. Sadly, the only animal that routinely kills elephants is man.)

A Mountain Out of a Molehill

The original wording was to make an elephant out of a fly, via the Greek satirist Lucian, who lived at the beginning of the Common Era. But in 1548 Nicholas Udall published *Paraphrase of Erasmus*, which included his opinion that "Sophists of Greece could through their copiousness make an elephant of a fly and a mountain of a molehill." Only the latter part of his sentence has survived into modern times.

Humble Pie

To eat humble pie is to declare one is wrong, whether one believes it or not (as to a boss, parent, etc.), or apologize for something said or done. The expression dates back to medieval times—explain to friends who think medieval's second half means evil that eval means time, for example, coeval means existing at the same time or someone your own age. In those days, after a deer hunt the choicest meat was served to the male head of the household, his relatives, and guests, with the rest going to servants and lesser or uninvited guests. Those parts—kidneys, liver, and heart—were called numbles or umbles and were baked into pies. Eventually numble and umble were confounded with humble. The names of these edible deer entrails comes from Latin *lumbus*, loin, which is also the root of lumbar, pertaining to the lower back.

Humble pie is symbolic, unlike shoofly pie, whose name reflects its being an open sugar pie with molasses filling that attracts flies which one has to keep shooing away.

Musk...

Musk, a major ingredient in perfumery, is a potently aromatic reddish-brown substance secreted by the male musk deer. "Musk" may have derived from the Sanskrit—nearly all European languages are members of the Indo-European linguistic family—*muska*, or scrotum, due to the similar shape of the deer's abdominal sac where musk is produced. Musk deer are a small East Asian deer without antlers.

The word musk is attached to animals and plants that smell musky—like the musk plant, related to the red or yellow monkey flower. (Nothing to do with musketeers, though the famous men's cologne Aramis is named after one of Alexandre Dumas's literary Musketeers.)

Once famous for its fashionable fur, the muskrat is a big semi-aquatic North American rodent that smells musky, while a musk ox is no ox, but a big goat-antelope with a horny projection on its head and a shaggy coat convenient for living in the tundra of North America and Greenland (whose name, as most readers know, is from colonial advertising rather than geographical fact).

The musk rose is also big, a musk-scented white rambling rose. ("Ramble" is said to be related to an Old Dutch word, *rammelen*, which referred to animals that "wander about on heat.")

Musquash is another name for muskrat, but in Britain means muskrat fur.

(Why do deer remain transfixed by an oncoming car's headlights? Stillness, a universal fear response, affords time to decide whether to fight or flee, though too much time may be fatal. Freezing is also a means to avoid detection—run, and the predator will pursue. Occasionally the unchallenged aggressor simply goes away.)

Buck and Naked

Buck, the male of certain animals, particularly deer, is from Olde English buc, a male deer, of Germanic origin and related to *bucca*, male goat. However, in South Africa a buck is an antelope of either sex.

A buck is also a vertical jump in which a horse lowers its head, arches its back and throws its back legs out behind.

The verb buck means to resist—such as to buck a trend. The adjective denotes the lowest of a given US military rank, like a buck private. The noun buck means responsibility, as in the phrases the buck stops here or passing the buck.

A buck, origin unknown, is a US dollar, also an Australian or New Zealand dollar, a South African rand, or an Indian rupee.

To buck someone up is to cheer them up. To buck up also means to become more hard-working or serious about something.

A buckboard is or was a North American four-wheeled, open horse-drawn carriage with seating attached to a plank between the front and rear axles.

A buck used also to mean a fashionable and daring young man, and before that a black male slave. Buck naked is said to derive from the related words buck and buff, the color of a buckskin and supposedly the pale tan color of European skin.

Buff, actually a yellowish beige color or a pad or cloth used to polish something, comes from French and Italian words born of the Latin for buffalo. When somebody is buffed, they're in great physical shape (often via a gym), and in the buff is slang for naked. Butt naked emphasizes the nudity.

Buffalo comes from a Greek word meaning antelope and wild ox. Due to the animal's size and temperament, to buffalo someone means to intimidate them. Also to trick or fool them, arising from US hunters' practice in the 1870s of sneaking up close enough to a herd to be able to pick individuals off.

Skunk

Odd that although a skunk's signature trait is the foul odor it protectively emits via its anal glands, when a human is called a skunk it hasn't to do with smell but moral quality. The Latin name of the skunk, a member of the weasel family, is *Mephitis*

mephitis, or noxious exhalation, related to Mephistopheles, the devil or evil spirit to whom Faust sold his soul in the German legend.

To skunk someone is US slang meaning, per the *Concise Oxford English Dictionary*, to "defeat or get the better of, especially by an overwhelming margin."

Skunk is also short for skunkweed, cannabis that includes a high concentration of narcotic agents. Skunk cabbage is a North American arum whose flowers frankly stink.

Skunkworks is a nickname for a small experimental laboratory or department of a company or organization, inspired by the Skonk Works, an illegal still in the once-popular comic strip "Li'l Abner."

Most of what little we know about skunks comes from cartoons. Skunks themselves are clean animals and don't stink—what they spray stinks. Some skunks give a warning of three stomps before they spray what they think is an aggressor. Courteous? Perhaps, but adult male skunks have been known to kill young skunks. Something Pepe le Pew would never do, *n'est-ce pas?*

Pepe's last name is no coincidence. In English, when something smells foul, we say p.u. In Latin, *puteo* means to stink, and the Indo-European word-root *pu* (also as in poo) denotes rot or decay. Several languages have words referring to bad smells that start with p-u. P.u., neither an abbreviation nor an acronym, became a word in the United States some time in the mid 20th century.

NON-MAMMALS

On Wings

Perhaps the animal most envied by humans, apart from a poodle on a pillow, is the bird, with its near-magical ability to fly. Numerous expressions have arisen around wings, most of them derived positionally after the horizontal projections from a main part that parallel a bird's wings. For instance, the wings of a building or theatrical stage. The latter produced the expression "to wing it," as in an unprepared actor trying to memorize lines while standing in the wings, then improvising on stage.

Today the phrase, which began in the late 1800s, doesn't usually involve a thespian. It took a long time to go wide; the November 1959 issue of *Esquire* magazine defined wing for its readers as "do something without preparation." A second current meaning is to adapt as one goes along, as in "I'll propose my version, see what the boss says, then wing it."

In the wings means ready for action or use when called or needed.

Wingbeat and wingspan are self-evident, as is on the wing, while on a wing and a prayer indicates almost no chance of success. Children as well as young birds stretch or try their wings, and kids may wear water wings in a swimming pool while learning to swim.

An older person may take a younger one under their wing, mentoring the youth and offering winged words, that is, appropriate or significant ones. The elder may wear a wing collar, whose turned-down corners resemble little bird wings, and wingtip shoes, whose toecap and sides call to mind (well, some minds) a wing.

(A word for the younger person is the older one's protégé, protected in French.)

A Dole of Doves

As with the famous but non-specific gaggle of geese, there are names for groups of specific animals. Some avian examples:

- a dole of doves
- a wedge of swans
- a bouquet of pheasants
- a charm of finches
- a company of plovers
- a kettle of hawks (not fish)
- a bevy of quail
- a murder of crows
- a descent of woodpeckers
- a peep of chickens
- a colony of penguins

The Birds and the Bees

The birds and the bees is a handy, sanitized way of semi-explaining sex to children. Especially at springtime, when both are easily seen—bees buzzing and pollinating and birds laying eggs and raising their young. Neither visual includes penetration (it's not the birds and the dogs ...), and the phrase is prettily alliterative. Tracing its first appearance is tricky, because some writers mentioned birds and bees in one work, but not together, or if in tandem, not as "the birds and the bees." In 1825 poet Samuel Taylor Coleridge wrote, "All nature seems at work ... The bees are stirring—birds are on the wing." In his 1928 song "Let's Do It, Let's Fall in Love," Cole Porter wrote that "Birds do it, bees do it, even educated fleas do it...." Some time in the 20th century the phrase became indelibly established in its present form, and in 1965 got a new lease on the facts of life via Jewel Akens's hit song "The Birds and the Bees."

More Wings

A wing chair has side projections from a high back; however, a three-way mirror isn't called a wing mirror, which is a rear-view mirror projecting from a car's side. A wing nut has small projections so one can turn it on a screw with one's fingers; it's also known as a butterfly nut.

Wingding, a lively party or youth-oriented happening (another very '60s word), dates back to the 1920s, when it meant a spasm or seizure, usually via drug-taking. That "roaring" (like a lion?) decade saw a wider distribution of drugs, especially cocaine, after the huge losses and disillusionment of World War I (or the Great War, since WWII was yet to come, and of course "Great" meaning big, not excellent).

In soccer and hockey a winger is an attacking player. A wingman is a pilot whose plane is positioned behind and outside a formation's lead aircraft. Wing commander is a Royal Air Force officer just below a group captain. Wing walking is—mostly was—performing acrobatics on the wing of an airborne craft. And a wingover, still seen at air shows, occurs when a pilot turns at the top of a steep climb and flies his plane back along its original route.

To wing someone with a firearm is to "merely" wound them in the arm or shoulder.

Left- and right-wing, politically, originated with France's National Assembly (1789–1791), where the nobles sat to the president's right and the commons to the left, the concept being that the former wanted to preserve rights for themselves while the latter wanted to grant rights to one and all.

(The first Academy Award for Best Picture was won by *Wings* [1927].)

Giving the Bird

The origins of to give or flip someone the bird are far from simple, partly because it goes back so far. The middle finger has been associated with the penis since at least ancient Greece (though in various cultures, like today's Iran and Afghanistan, the thumb fills the same role). The Greeks also associated the penis with birds, one reason being the "nest" of pubic hair. In the West, certain birds have a long literary history of taunting other animals or humans. Hunters' and soldiers' arrows were sometimes compared to lethal birds. In the Middle Ages the French considered cutting off the middle fingers of English soldiers captured in France so they could no longer draw their longbows, which often used pheasant feathers. The expression to flip the bird is as recent as the 1960s, but the first photographed instance of same is an 1886 group photo of the Boston Beaneaters baseball team in which a pitcher is flashing his middle finger.

Getting the bird, seldom heard today, refers to someone, typically a performer, being rejected, usually by an audience. That is, they boo or hiss him, supposedly sounding like a hissing flock of geese. The original expression was to get the big bird. (On *Sesame Street*, Big Bird has a happy audience.)

Speaking of giving each other the bird, the term war hawk was coined by Thomas Jefferson in 1798 but the modern distinction between hawks and doves, used so often during the Vietnam war of the 1960s and early '70s, dates only from the 1962 Cuban missile crisis.

Feathers

The meaning of to ruffle someone's feathers is obvious, and a feather in one's cap comes from the Native American custom of awarding a feather to a courageous brave, as well as European traditions of adding ostrich or other feathers to winning warriors' crests since at least the 1300s. Contrarily, starting in the 1700s a white feather was given to a man considered a coward or one who hadn't enlisted in the military. This derived from the idea that a white feather in a game bird's tail signified bad breeding.

But you could have knocked me over with a feather? Australian ornithologist Shelly Cantrell offers, "Assertions of surprise have long used animal imagery, but a diary that my great-grandmother kept in England said this one was new … it was much in vogue with her girlfriends yet disapproved of by most adults, presumably because it was a bit on the sensuous side."

Featherbedding originally meant excessively generous or easy working conditions that made a job as comfortable as a feather-stuffed mattress. Today it means overstaffing, not stuffing—too many people employed for the work required (a common practice in Third World countries, to hold down unemployment and unrest).

Today birds of a feather merely connotes that like usually attracts like. Having things and attitudes and goals in common tends to bind any relationship. But centuries ago the phrase was derogatory, denoting that unsavory individuals—criminals, gamblers, promiscuous sorts, etc.—gather together in the same place.

To fly off the handle, or get upset, derives from medieval times when impatient falcons, kestrels, and other birds would fly off their "handles" or their owners' gloved hands in search of prey.

By the way, birds don't sweat. They haven't any sweat glands. The most common ways they cool off are panting—like a dog, but much quieter—and ruffling their feathers, which lets in air and helps get rid of excess heat. (Reptiles, evolutionarily once related to birds, don't sweat either.)

Ostrich

A ratite is a bird with a flat breastbone and no keel (a central ridge along the back or convex surface of an organ). Thus it cannot fly. The word has nothing to do with rats. Ostriches are ratites and do not bury their heads in the sand, an expression dating back to the Romans or before, symbolizing avoiding or denying an unpleasant reality. Rather, when ostriches sense approaching danger they put their long necks parallel to the ground and listen closely. If they feel threatened, ostriches can speed away at 40 miles (about 60 kilometers) per hour—they grow up to nine feet (2.74 meters) tall and 300 pounds (136 kg.), yet are quite agile.

The incorrect expression may also have developed because ostrich nests are just depressions scraped in the sand, and when mama tends to her eggs she lowers her little head way down. Nor are ostriches scaredy-cats, to coin a phrase. They're formidable foes with sharp beaks and extremely powerful legs.

Birds...

Most avian expressions are self-explanatory, like free as a bird, a bird's-eye view, the early bird gets the worm, or to kill two birds with one stone (fortunately usually impossible). Bird is also used to denote a specific type of person, for example, a jailbird or a rare bird or a tough old bird. A home bird prefers to stay in rather than go out. In Britain bird is the equivalent of American chick in regard to a young woman. Dolly bird is British slang for a good-looking but supposedly stupid young woman.

A golf birdie, as in a hole played in one stroke under par, derives from the 19th-century use of bird as slang for something good or excellent. In 1899 or 1921, depending on the source, an Atlantic City golfer said of a particularly good shot that it was a bird; his fellow players took up and amended the word to birdie. An eagle is a big birdie and a double eagle is three under par—and exceedingly rare.

Signifying an unnameable source, the expression a little bird told me goes back to the Bible. (Of course a little bird is a birdie.)

The bird has flown means the individual you sought has disappeared. "The birds have flown," declared Charles I in the 17th century when he and his soldiers arrived at the House of Commons too late to arrest his political adversaries.

One swallow does not make a summer goes back to ancient Greece and has equivalents in many languages. It usually warns not to arrive at a hasty conclusion or make too much of a single experience or episode.

Side note: Ever wonder why many birds sleep standing on one leg? First, their locking toes allow them to perch—one or two legs—on a telephone wire without falling off. Second, because they've no feathers on their feet, birds can lose body heat standing on cold surfaces or in cold water. To preserve energy they stand on just one leg. They also stick their heads under their feathers to conserve heat.

Chicks to Tits

Chick is a Middle English abbreviation of chicken, now usually denoting a young chicken or young woman. Not all words beginning with chick- are of fowl origin. For instance chickweed, chickpea (also known as garbanzo), and chickaree, a red-furred squirrel found in coniferous North American forests named for the sound of its call. Chick lit is fiction aimed at young women, chick flicks have the same target audience, and chicken feed is a negligible amount of money.

But a chicken brick is a pottery container for roasting a chicken in its own juices and chickadee is the North American name—also supposedly imitative of its call—for a tit or titmouse. Despite the name(s), a tit or titmouse is a small songbird that searches for food acrobatically among branches and foliage. Originally a titmose, its second syllable morphed into mouse. In Britain it's more often called a tit, which also means a foolish person. As for tit for tat, that never had to do with the bird—it's a 16th-century variation of the original tip for tat.

For the Birds' Brain

Before there were automobiles, people riding in carts and carriages sometimes complained about the smell and bother of horsesh*t. Post-equus, people sometimes complain about birdsh*t, specifically droppings onto windshields or car bodies. "For the birds" is said to be shortened US Army slang devised toward the end of World War II, originally: "That's sh*t for the birds," that is, something worthless or worse.

Speaking of which, the dark dot in the middle of those white droppings is avian poo; the white is its sticky urine. Birds have no sphincter muscles and do #1 and 2 at the same time, from the same orifice. Is this too much information?

Birdbrain was a judgment both biased—small animal, small brain—and precipitate, prior to studies of birds' brains (relatively big for their size) and their behavior. Animal intelligence is measured partly by successful adaptation to one's environment—and birds have existed far longer than humans—plus factors such as tool use, which is known to several birds.

To eat like a bird is another misnomer, still current in the age of anorexia. If anything, birds tend toward necessary gluttony, requiring extra energy to sustain flight.

A harpy is a scolding or unpleasant woman. In Greek mythology harpies, meaning snatchers, were large birds with women's faces and breasts who snatched food from tables and deliberately made an awful mess. (A harpy eagle is a crested eagle living in tropical rainforests.) Harridan, another sexist term for a disliked woman, may derive from a French word for an old horse.

Sirens, now betokening alluring women, were mythological nymphs whose sweet song drove men mad and to destruction. Sirens were often depicted as birds with beautiful women's faces. In ancient times—Greek, biblical, etc.—women were often presented as destructive and frequently given animal traits.

Jaywalker

Jays, members of the crow family, usually with blue feathers, thrived along the east coast of what is now the US when European colonists arrived. As more and more arrived, most jays withdrew to the country. By the mid 1700s jay was a nickname for a country bumpkin. Rural visitors to growing cities were often baffled by the traffic, not knowing where or when to cross the street, and sometimes doing so without looking. By the early 20th century a jaywalker was what he or she is now. Today they really should know better.

A Regular Aviary

A coot is a black aquatic bird with a white bill that ascends onto its forehead as a horny shield. Calling a man a coot or old coot originally meant he was stupid or eccentric. Because coots have a featherless pate on the forehead that looks like an old man's head, old coot became a derogatory term for an elderly man—and yielded the phrase "as bald as a coot," or completely bald. (After Vivian Vance met the much older William Frawley, who was to play Ethel Mertz's husband Fred on *I Love Lucy*, she told Lucille Ball, "Who's ever going to believe I'd be married to that old coot?" Frawley overheard her, and the feud was on.)

Because larks are songbirds that seem cheerful, rise early (unlike night owls) and even sing on the wing, their associations are upbeat—to be up with the lark, to be happy as a lark, to lark about, to be larky, or to have a lark or do something for a lark.

Big, black, and raucous, crows have a contrasting image to larks. To crow over something is to gloat unattractively. An old crow is an ugly old woman. Crow's feet—sounds more dramatic than, say, sparrow's feet—eventually show up around men's and women's eyes. A crowbar's splayed grappling end was said, by the 15th century, to resemble a crow's foot or its beak. As the crow flies is a theoretical straight line between two points.

Four-and-twenty black birds, from the nursery rhyme, reminds us that once upon a time English, like German today, reverse-ordered numbers between twenty and one hundred.

Pigeons

This gray, usually larger relative of the dove has a very different image from the generally white, more delicate bird. A pigeon is a gullible individual, sometimes a scam victim. Pigeon-hearted signifies timid or cowardly.

Pigeon-toed means toes or feet turned inwards. Pigeon-chested or -breasted indicates a narrow, protruding chest.

In Britain one's pigeon is one's business or responsibility.

A pigeon pair meant girl-and-boy twins or a boy and girl as a family's sole children, back when having "just" two was atypical.

Pigeon's milk—better you don't ask—is a curd-like secretion from a pigeon's crop* (the pouch in a bird's gullet in which food is stored or prepared for digestion) that it regurgitates and feeds to its offspring. A pouter pigeon can significantly inflate its crop.

A pigeon pea is a tropical red pea-like seed or the plant which produces it, used as fodder. Pigeon pie is slang for pigeon as an entrée, which it is in poorer countries such as Egypt.

A pigeonhole was first a small compartment for a pigeon to nest in. Then it was a small compartment in a desk. Then it came to mean placing someone into a restrictive category that kept their career or outlook small—as for example actors pigeonholed into playing only villains, kooky neighbors, or bird-brained blondes.

*Jabot, a French word used in English, means a bird's crop but is the ornamental ruffle on the front of a shirt or blouse.

…Beating Around the Bush

The expression "the game is up" doesn't derive from an old sporting event, but from hunting. Aristocrats hunting game on their country estates employed beaters to drive pheasants and other game birds out of their nests or hiding places and into the open. The beaters would yell, "The game is up!" to inform their employers that the birds were exposed and the shooting could begin.

That's also the origin of beating around the bush, since beating branches and making noise flushed the game from the bush, allowing hunters to avoid directly approaching their quarry. This was routine for bird and boar hunting—to scare birds into the open, sometimes catching them in nets, and to avoid the surprise of a boar's razor-sharp tusks or being charged. The practice was also called bushwhacking, but the original phrase was probably to beat *about* the bush, as it still is in Britain.

The possible first mention of the phrase was circa 1440 in the anonymous medieval poem "Generydes—A Romance in

Seven-line Stanzas": "beting the bussh" (almost no standard-ization of spelling yet). In his 1572 *Works* George Gascoigne was the first to write "beat about the bush."

Aviary II

Round robin now usually means a sporting tournament in which a player plays every other player in turn—a round-robin competition. Its earliest use, in the 16th century, was a nick-name for a devious person. In the mid 17th century a round robin was a Roundhead, a supporter of Parliament in the Eng-lish Civil War. Later it became a petition of complaint—often by sailors aboard ship—whose signatures formed a circle so to conceal the order of writing and not indicate a ringleader who could be held accountable and punished.

In Britain, "sick as a parrot" means being appalled by the outcome of a soccer (football) game. The phrase apparently became widespread after 1973, when several people in West Africa died of psittacosis, a viral disease of parrots and other birds that had rarely been transmitted to humans. The origi-nal expression may have been "sick as a parrot with a rubber beak," denoting—like "a cat in hell without claws"—an ani-mal left defenseless without a sharp weapon.

To quail, meaning to be afraid or apprehensive, has noth-ing to do with the cute little plump bird. And a culture vul-ture is a person avid for culture, which in a TV-oriented soci-ety is considered somewhat extreme.

Since ancient times the albatross, a very big seabird from the southern oceans, has been considered a bird of ill omen, in part because of its size and ability to successfully compete with fishermen. An albatross around one's neck is a great burden—like a monkey on one's back—very difficult to get rid of. The most famous example is in Coleridge's 1798 poem "The Rime of the Ancient Mariner." Albatross derives from Latin *albus*, white, and Spanish *alcatraz* (like the former San Francisco prison), which means gannet or its relative the pelican, but also a calla lily(!).

Many gulls aren't seagulls, though we tend to think of them all as such and are often surprised to see one many miles inland or a bunch of "sea" gulls standing in the middle of a shopping-center parking lot (where there's lots of litter for them to choose from). A gull is also a person who's fooled or deceived; to gull is to fool or deceive. And gull-wings on a car or aircraft open upwards.

Turkey

Native to North America, for thousands of years this was a primary food source for inhabitants and, later, colonizers. Turkeys were introduced to Europe in the 1500s by Spaniards who "discovered" them in Mexico, where today's word for turkey is via the Aztecs, while in Spain another word is used. Cows, pigs, and horses were introduced to the Americas by the *conquistadores*.

Ben Franklin argued strongly for adopting the turkey as the United States' national bird. However, the eagle—a bird of prey and symbol of conquest since at least the Roman empire—got the nod. (India's national bird is the stunning peacock, and peacock butterflies likewise boast prominent "eyes.")

The name "turkey" comes from the dissimilar guineafowl, which was exported to Europe through Turkey and usually called a Turkey hen or Turkey cock. North American colonists somehow confused the birds and called the native after the Mideastern nation from which neither bird came.

Although most expressions involving turkey are negative, there is a positive one: in bowling, achieving three strikes in a row is called a turkey. The term may have originated because of holiday-time tournaments in which competitors bowling three strikes against the heavier pins—typically four pounds—won a live turkey.

Turkey Shoot to Turkey Vultures

The plight of the vulnerable turkey is invoked in this first North American term referring to a situation, particularly in war, wherein the aggressor has a tremendous advantage and the outcome is a virtually foregone conclusion.

A turkey oak is a southern European oak with a domed fanning crown and acorn cups featuring feather-like out-pointing long scales.

The turkey trot, not likely to be confused with the less jolly foxtrot, was a popular 20th-century ballroom dance performed to ragtime music.

The turkey vulture is easily the most common vulture in North America, found in Canada, all 50 US states and Mexico. It's often mistakenly called a buzzard, a hawk-like bird of prey whose name is from the Latin for falcon. Like other vultures, it doesn't circle soon-to-be-dead prey. Rather, it conserves energy by soaring in circles, sometimes for hours, on thermals—updrafts of warm rising air—while flapping its wings as little as possible. (Yet again, movies, TV, and cartoons often ignore the truth for dramatic effect and stereotyping, which is a form of shorthand.)

A vulture won't land until it's certain its intended meal is dead and there's minimal competition from land creatures or other birds; vultures are basically passive. A prime means of defending themselves is projectile vomiting, up to ten feet's worth of malodorous carrion aimed at a soon-to-be-disgusted enemy.

Talking Turkey

Radical shifts of meaning in words are frequently more explainable than in phrases. In the late 1700s to talk turkey meant to chat (short for chatter, often applied to birds and monkeys). Conversely, to "not say turkey" or "not say pea-turkey" meant not to talk at all, to keep silent.

Why turkeys were associated with speech is a mystery, though their gobbling reminded some people of conversation. Also, turkeys are sociable birds that congregate in flocks, the males sometimes courting in pairs(!). Because turkeys were so abundant, so easy to kill, and so delicious to eat, it was sometimes said that most conversations between the Pilgrims and Native Americans involved "talking about turkey."

It's also been reported that turkey hunters could attract a bird's attention by making gobble-gobble sounds, imitating the poor turkey, which answered back and alerted its foe to its presence.

Regardless, by the early 20th century, to talk turkey had shifted from casual conversation to discussing cold, hard facts. Today it often has a business connotation, as in "Call my attorney when you're ready to talk turkey."

The Parson's Nose

The fleshy bump on the end of a dressed turkey is called a pygostyle—chickens, ducks, and geese also have one—covering the join where the avian spine and tail feathers attach. The pygostyle's fatted appearance is due to oil glands a bird uses when preening. To somebody with an influence on the English language, this protuberance resembled a snooty up-turned nose and so, depending whom one preferred to insult, it was called the parson's nose, pope's nose, or sultan's nose. The phrase goes back to the Middle Ages, when religion ruled the roost.

A roost isn't just where birds settle to rest at night, it's also where bats settle to rest in the day.

Going Cold Turkey

At first, one didn't do something cold turkey, one *talked* cold turkey (related to "talking turkey"). As in a 1922 letter by poet Carl Sandburg: "I'm going to talk cold turkey with booksellers."

Cold turkey was also a slangy adverb-equivalent for suddenly. Example: "I made one mistake, then found myself out of a job cold turkey."

By the 1930s cold turkey was addict slang for sudden narcotics withdrawal, and was listed as such in a 1936 article in *American Speech*. The skin of someone withdrawing from drugs is said to be pale, clammy, and prone to goose bumps, like the skin of a plucked turkey (but not a plucked goose?). Author William Burroughs, no stranger to substance abuse, observed in *Junkie* (1953) that one's skin during withdrawal looks like a turkey's that's been plucked, cooked, and left out to cool.

Or the expression may hark back to 1910, when comparison was made between a cold turkey meal requiring minimal preparation and withdrawing from drug use with no preparation. As the century dragged on, cold turkey became most closely associated with quitting smoking (and was the title of a 1971 Dick Van Dyke movie in which an entire town gives up smoking).

Nowadays cold turkey may also refer to sudden relinquishing of less hazardous habits like cheesecake, ice cream, cookies, or chocolate!

N.B. Yes, Latin—*nota bene*, note well: Although dark chocolate is healthier for humans than milk chocolate, it's often lethal for small dogs, due to the ingredient theobromine, which ironically means (from the Greek) food of the gods. *Caveat emptor.*

The Goose That Laid the Golden Egg

To kill the goose that lays the golden egg is to be self-destructively greedy and shortsighted. In 1484 William Caxton translated Aesop's famous fable in which an uneducated peasant discovers a goose that lays golden eggs. One golden egg fills the man with impatient greed, so he kills the animal to retrieve her remaining eggs. The moral is to not be carried away by greed and to consider the long- rather than the short-term.

Nest Egg

Today a nest egg is typically someone's savings or a sum set aside for the future, but originally it meant something to add to, specifically, an inducement. Before corporate farming, when hens could roam about and lay their eggs in nests, people still sought greater productivity. To encourage it, a farmer might put a porcelain or pottery egg, called a nest egg, into the nest. It often worked. Similarly, a small gift of money presented to someone as a "nest egg" was meant to encourage them to add to it. One example popular in the prospering years after World War II was to give a child a piggy bank containing some—not too many—pleasingly noisy coins.

Speaking of money, a dollarbird is an Australasian roller with a distinctive white coin-like mark on its wing. A roller is a brightly colored crow-sized bird, mostly blue, with a typically tumbling display flight. It's also a type of canary with a trilling sound and a breed of tumbler pigeon.

Bird's Nest Soup

In Hong Kong a bowl of bird's nest soup can be had for the equivalent of $30 to $100. Sound expensive? To buy bird nest by the kilo costs about $2,500. But the nests of swiftlets, small swifts native to South Asia and Australasia, aren't the usual avian home built of twigs. Rather, swiftlets, thanks to oversized salivary glands, fabricate their nests with interwoven strings of gluey saliva that act like cement but which, when dissolved in water, have a gelatinous texture. Bird's nest soup has been a Chinese delicacy for over 400 years and remains popular with those who can afford it. Predictably, it's reputed to have medicinal and aphrodisiacal qualities.

A Wild Goose Chase

This expression dates back to 16th-century England and the bizarre beginnings of horse racing. To wit, a lead horse would run off in whatever direction the rider chose. After a delay, a second horse and rider would pursue, followed at regular intervals by more of same. But since none of the subsequent riders knew what route the first horse and rider had taken, they dispersed variously, which reminded somebody of the assorted directions taken by wild geese flocking after their leader.

The English associated the phrase with horse racing until Shakespeare changed the meaning to fruitless pursuit. In *Romeo and Juliet* (1597) Mercutio declares, "Nay, if our wits run the wild-goose Chase, I am done."

Today a wild goose chase is a fruitless pursuit or an empty errand or process one is sent on by a devious sender to buy him time (especially in the movies).

Goosestep

What has the notorious goosestep to do with a goose? After all, geese bend their (backward-pointing) knees when they walk. Once again, the English name wasn't the original when the step was introduced into the army of militaristic Prussia (northern Germany) in the mid 1700s. It was called *Stechschritt*, stabbing step. Somebody thought the marching step resembled that of a goose, but the German term *Gaensemarch*, or goose march, couldn't be used, as it already meant people, especially children, walking in single file—like goslings after their mother. In the early 1800s Britain began calling it the goosestep. When the French named it, it was *pas de l'oie* (goosestep). Italians called it *passo Romano* (Roman step).

The aggressive step, with legs raised high and knees unbent, was meant to intimidate and give an impression of extreme uniformity—a definition of fascism; the step became indelibly associated in the 1920s with Mussolini's Fascists and in the '30s with Hitler's Nazis.

Gooseflesh

It's called gooseflesh, gooseskin, goosebumps, and goose pimples—also *cutis anserina*, the latter word the adjective pertaining to geese. Intense cold or extreme fear and excitement, including sexual pleasure or awe, can cause involuntary bumps at the base of human body hairs. A pertinent but barely known word is horripilation, the erection of hairs on the skin due to those usually unexpected and strong emotions. The term comes from the Latin for horrible and hair.

A classic musical composition is "Capriccio Espagnol." A capriccio is a lively piece of music, but was also a 17th-century name for a fantasy painting that may have included elements of horror. Related to the word caprice, which used to have darker connotations, it's Italian from *capo*, head, and *riccio*, hedgehog, referring to that animal's spiny hair standing frightfully on end.

Human gooseflesh may be a vestigial response—the rising of hair to make the body seem larger and more formidable to an adversary. This occurs in many mammals, including cats and sea otters when they see sharks. As for geese, their feathers grow from stores in their skin that look like human hair follicles; when a goose's feathers are plucked, its skin has protrusions where the feathers were—ergo, goose bumps. This phenomenon, seen in various other birds, is also known as arasing, piloerection, and the pilomotor reflex (from *pilus*, Latin for hair; *pelo* means hair in Spanish, for instance).

Non-Goose

Never heard of goosefoot? It's an edible plant whose divided leaves supposedly resemble a goose's foot. Known as very nutritious in the Midwest and increasingly popular in salads everywhere, the plural is goosefoots. But you already know the most famous member of the goosefoot family: spinach.

Goosegrass is a widespread plant related to bedstraws (previously used to stuff mattresses).

Gooseberry is an edible round berry, usually reddish or yellowish-green, with a thin, translucent, fuzzy skin. A British name for it is goosegog.

In Britain a gooseberry is also a third wheel, a third person whom two people would rather shed to be alone together. To play gooseberry is to be a chaperone, for the gooseberry is a traditional symbol of anticipation. When children asked where babies came from, parents often said they were found underneath a gooseberry bush, an explanation that endured into the 1920s.

A gooseneck is a pipe or support curved like a goose's neck.

A goose egg is North American slang for a zero score in a game.

A goosefish is a North American bottom-dwelling anglerfish.

A goose barnacle is a stalked barnacle that hangs from floating objects in water and catches passing food with its feathery legs.

A silly goose is somebody foolish or hopeless, and a gone goose (or gone gosling) is someone for whom there's no hope, for example, "He hasn't kept his grades up—he's a gone goose for entering Harvard."

Never heard of goose-dirt shoes? They're seldom mentioned today, but on the Internet there's a whole photographic array of the casual, sometimes colorful footwear.

Geese...

"What's sauce for the goose is sauce for the gander" (a male goose), now a retort to the double standard, was originally a 17th-century cooking term meaning female geese and ganders didn't have to be cooked differently or separately (duh). A gannet, a big seabird that catches fish by plunge-diving, is linguistically related to gander, which was criminal slang; gannet is current British slang for a greedy individual. (To take or have a gander is to take a look, said to reflect anserine curiosity.)

A goose is also a tailor's smoothing iron.

To goose someone is to poke them. (Q: If you poke a goose, are you giving it a person?) It originally meant to poke someone in the bottom, as geese are wont to do. Though sociable amongst themselves, geese frequently bite people, their beaks reaching about the height of a person's bottom. To give someone a goose now means to poke or elbow them anywhere, often in the side.

"Gay as a goose" is mostly explained by alliteration. Over 100 animal species also practice homosexuality; however, it's more prevalent in higher animals, specifically mammals, than birds—notwithstanding the lesbian seagulls made famous in song by Engelbert Humperdinck. Though the 20th-century phrase usually referred to homosexuality, some sources say it referred to merry, cheerful geese. If so, again alliteration played a substantial role.

To cook someone's goose is to dramatically deal an opponent a crushing blow. To cook one's goose is to do something that backfires on one. The former expression is said to date back to the Middle Ages, when an army prepared to attack a confidently prosperous town whose leaders hung a goose outside the city gate as a sign of contempt. The affronted army burned down the town and "cooked its goose."

A goshawk is a short-winged hawk whose Olde English name meant goose hawk.

Somebody unable to say boo to a goose is excessively shy or timid.

Mother Goose was and is the archetypal teller of children's nursery rhymes. She's sometimes depicted as a goose, sometimes as a human wearing a Welsh hat that looks witch-y but is offset by her friendly expression.

FYI, geese mate for life and grieve at a mate's loss. If a goose becomes sick or is wounded in flight, two geese will leave the formation to escort and protect the goose, remaining with it until it dies or is able to fly on its own.

Cuckold and Cuckoo

Cuckold, a man whose wife cheats on him, comes from cuckoo, a bird that lays her eggs in another bird's nest. Why would she do such a cuckoo thing?

First, cuckoo was coined by the 1200s, the name imitative of the bird's call. By the 1500s the word could describe a foolish person, as people at the time were unaware that the she-cuckoo is deviously clever rather than foolish. She chooses another bird's eggs that resemble her own, then removes a few from the foreign nest so the host bird won't push the cuckoo's eggs out.

By the 13th century cuckold referred to a man with an unfaithful wife, for in addition to the female cuckoo's oviparous habits, she often has more than one mate and doesn't settle down to one single nest (the phrase "free as a bird" comes to mind).

The cuckold was said—particularly in Mediterranean cultures—to "wear the horns," referencing not birds, but stags, who lock horns in battle. The defeated male cedes his mate to the victor. The sign of the horn, made with the second and fifth fingers, is still used in many countries, and in Sicily it's a grave insult to call a man a cuckold.

By the early 1900s and especially in the United States, cuckoo came to mean somebody crazy. In keeping with the trend to shorter words, "kook" emerged from cuckoo in the late 1950s but like its adjective kooky, had a softer meaning: somebody offbeat or colorful, not necessarily nuts.

Cuckoos

Cuckoo bees are parasitic (not all bees work hard), laying their eggs in the nest of another sort of bee, while cuckoo wasps lay theirs in nests of other wasps or bees.

The cuckooflower has pale lilac flowers that bloom in spring, when the male cuckoo's distinctive, far-carrying two-note call is first heard. "The Dance of the Cuckoos" was the signature tune of the immortal movie comedy team Laurel and Hardy.

A cuckoo pint is a widespread wild arum with a green or purple spadix and red berries. It was formerly called a cuckoo-pintle (sic), from Olde English pintel (sic), or penis, via the shape of the spadix. (How many people know that *penis* is Latin for tail?)

Cuckoo spit is a pale froth extruded onto leaves and plant stems by the larvae of froghoppers.

And who hasn't heard a cuckoo clock?

Crazy as a Loon?

The word lunatic descends from the Latin *luna*, moon, for many ancient peoples held that overexposure to moonlight caused madness. Loony means silly or mad, someone who perhaps belongs in a loony bin. Loony is also slang for the Canadian dollar coin, after the avian loon depicted on it. The bird's name is from Scandinavian *lom*, clumsy. The Olde English word loun, meaning madman or clown, evolved into the Scottish loon, a simpleton or crazy person.

How did the bird become identified with craziness? Human judgment. Expert swimmers who can dive as deep as 250 feet beneath the surface to catch food, loons are clumsy on land, their legs positioned well back on their bodies. They have trouble becoming airborne from land or water. They also rear straight up in the water, flapping their wings while moving horizontally to scare off intruders. Then there are the calls of the loon, some comparable to the laugh of a madman and most sounding peculiar to human ears (some are audible up to two miles away). Each call has a meaning to the loon issuing it, and to other loons.

The loon got its name in the early 1600s. The expression crazy as a loon spread among European settlers in North America—in Britain the bird is called a diver—and by the late 1800s, loony was slang for nuts. However, there are loon fossils from 20 million years ago, and their ancestry goes back about 70 million years. Loons—or divers—are among the oldest, therefore most successful, living birds. How crazy is that?

To Lay an Egg

Why this is considered a bad thing (it's good when chickens do it) is unknown. Sources say it could be related to calling a failed play a "turkey," which has been widespread since the 1920s and occurs in Irving Berlin's song "There's No Business Like Show Business." The most famous use of the expression was *Variety*'s headline on October 30, 1929, referring to the previous day: "Wall Street Lays an Egg." It explained, "The most dramatic event in the financial history of America is the collapse of the New York Stock Market."

The term was borrowed from show business, and *Variety*, founded in 1905, is *the* entertainment newspaper of record.

Proof that the expression was little known outside showbiz was that it went virtually unused in any other coverage of the stock market crash. The *Variety* mention may have been the expression's first appearance in print, except for one other that year, a line in J. P. McEvoy's *Hollywood Girl*—"Boys, it looks like we laid an egg."

Again, why a fertilized ovum became associated with a public flop or disaster remains a mystery, but not every showbiz egg has referred to a "turkey." When double-Oscar-winner Jodie Foster formed her own production company, she named it Egg because an egg is a female product and is self-contained. Back when Jodie was still in the closet, comedy doyenne Dame Edna Everage, referring to Foster's fluency in French, called her a "cunning little linguist." (If you don't understand that, it's simple: Dame is the female equivalent of Sir, each having been knighted by the Queen, and a queen is either a king's wife or a female monarch. Simple?)

Laying Eggs

During World War I (1914–1918) fighter pilots created the slang term laying eggs, for dropping bombs. Referencing of course the bombs' shape and their being ejected from a plane's belly. If it was one bomb, the pilot may have said he laid an egg.

Speaking of bombs, the expression that a show or performer bombed (or failed, related to the preceding egg entry) was unknown during either world war. It gained popular currency in the 1960s.

P.S. One reason this writer won on *Jeopardy!* in 1998 was when I first visited Quebec, Canada, I read that animal pelts had long ago been common currency there, that is, used as money. My "Final *Jeopardy!*" category was Financial History.

(Pelt derives from Olde English pellet, meaning skin.)

Don't Count Your Chickens

Again, Aesop gets the credit, ca. 570 BCE. Everyone knows the expression means to not count on something prematurely or desire something too strongly before it's a possibility. But the story "The Milkmaid and Her Pail" is a little more complex than that. In it, the farmer's daughter daydreams while walking to market with a pail of milk balanced on her head. She imagines the milk will yield cream which she'll turn into butter which she'll sell at market, then buy several eggs that will hatch into chickens that will lay more eggs so she'll have a big poultry yard, then sell some of the hens and purchase a beautiful dress to visit the fair in, where the boys will dance attention upon her but she'll merely toss her head and ignore them. Daydreaming this, she tosses her head and loses the original pail of milk. Back home, Mama consoles and warns her, "Don't count your chickens before they're hatched."

The even more practical don't put all your eggs in one basket is much more recent, dating from the 18th century.

FYI: The reason some chickens lay white eggs and others brown has to do with a hen's breed. White eggs are far more popular, though both eggs' quality is the same. An easy way to gauge the color of a hen's eggs is her earlobes: if they're white, so are her eggs; if red, her eggs will be brown. An egg yolk's color depends on what the chicken is fed. If she eats white corn, her yolks will be colorless, but that's unpopular, so her diet is designed to produce yellow to orange yolks.

Egg...

An egg tooth is a tough white protuberance on the beak or jaw of an embryonic bird or reptile which facilitates its breaking out of the shell.

Egg roll is an odd name for a Chinese appetizer whose crisp deep-fried dough is made with eggs—on that basis, the names of countless foods could start with "egg." Egg rolls are often incorrectly labeled spring rolls, which are filled pancakes. (A springtail is a teeny wingless insect which springs upward when alarmed.)

Hundred-year-old eggs aren't really that old, but have been coated in an ash, rice, or lime mixture, then left—often buried—for up to six months. Even so, most Chinese house-wives who order them ask that they be delivered "fresh." Tea eggs are hard-boiled and soaked in tea to produce a delicate marbled effect.

(Years ago, at an ice cream parlor, I asked the difference between the flavors vanilla and the pricier French vanilla. I was coolly informed, "French vanilla has eggs." I felt like saying I didn't realize the French had invented eggs.)

Good Egg, Bad Egg

An egg may look fine on the outside but be rotten inside the shell, like some humans. In the same way that bird, duck, or party, etc., may refer to an individual ("She's a strange bird," "He's an odd duck"), so does egg—positively or negatively. In *Charlie and the Chocolate Factory* and its film versions Verruca Salt, a spoiled young heiress, gets dumped down a chute because she's a bad egg.

The phrase "a bad egg" first saw print in 1855 in Samuel A. Hammett's novel *Captain Priest*: "In the language of his class the Perfect Bird generally turns out to be a bad egg." By the 20th century the phrase was also being used positively, as in "Joe's a pretty good egg."

FYI, Grade AA eggs are "general purpose with thick whites and firm yolks that are virtually free from defects." Grade A eggs are "also general purpose but may have a defect or two." Grade B eggs are "not usually sold at retail but are usable for general cooking and baking." (USDA ratings of fruits and vegetables are A, B, and C.)

A dozen Extra Large eggs must weigh at least 27 ounces. A dozen Large eggs must weigh at least 24 ounces. A dozen Medium eggs must weigh at least 21 ounces. Egg-cellent information?

Egg-less

To egg someone on, that is, to urge or incite them to do something (often foolish or risky) derives not from edible eggs but the Old Norse *eggja*, "to incite." Likewise, an egg cream doesn't involve eggs but, rather, milk, soda water, and flavored syrup. And eggplant is a North American name for aubergine, which is also the vegetable's color—actually it's a fruit, eaten as a vegetable.

An egghead is an intellectual. In days of old ("when knights were bold and teachers weren't invented …") it was commonly thought the human brain could hold only so much knowledge. This anti-learning epithet implies that "excessive" reading or studying might expand the head upwards into an ovoid shape! Agatha Christie often described her brilliant Belgian detective Hercules Poirot as having an egg-shaped head. (Better an egghead than a Humpty-Dumpty.)

As Sure as Eggs

"As sure as eggs is eggs," though grammatically incorrect, expresses absolute certainty. But it's a misquote of the basic mathematical formula "x is x," stating complete certitude. How x became eggs sounds obvious, but when is uncertain, although Charles Dickens helped popularize the phrase in his 1837 novel *The Pickwick Papers*.

"Don't teach your grandmother to suck eggs" is almost obsolete but means "don't try to teach your elders something they probably already know." The expression reflected the practicality of toothless people eating eggs, raw or otherwise. In time, with more dentistry and a wider diet, the expression was partly replaced by the contemptuous "go suck an egg" uttered to comic effect by Cloris Leachman in an early episode of her TV sitcom *Phyllis*.

Pecking

To hen-peck is what a hen theoretically does to a rooster with her bill—technically it should be rooster-peck. For humans, it refers to a husband whose "hen" habitually pecks or picks on him, that is, she rules the roost. Philologist Mario Pei explained, "Although the verb to peck is of unknown source, 'peck' may come from a root meaning to protrude." Pecker in the United States is vulgar slang for a penis, while in Britain it means chin—both typically protrude—as in the expression keep your pecker up (which, when British officers used it during World War II radio broadcasts to encourage Yank soldiers, was usually censored).

Pecking order has been observed among hens, but also applies to humans and many or most species. Peckish, chiefly British, means hungry, though not ravenous. On both sides of the Atlantic, to peck at one's food indicates one's not very hungry.

The name of the red-bellied woodpecker, which bears a patch of red on the back of its head and neck—hence, a redneck—was reversed into peckerwood, which became a derogatory Southern US term for a poor white person, later largely supplanted by white trash and then joined by trailer trash.

Ever wondered why woodpeckers don't get headaches with all that banging against trees? They not only have specially thick skulls, but those that peck most often have skulls that curve inward at the upper base of the bill, so the skull isn't attached to the bill. The space between skull and bill is a natural shock absorber.

Hen...

Mad as a wet hen has more origin stories than some hens have eggs, but derives partly from the angry-seeming ruffling of feathers after a hen is splashed with water—something few creatures, including humans, would like—and from the cute or whimsical image of a hen upset.

Hen refers to the female of a domestic fowl, yet hens may refer to domestic fowls of either sex, and a native hen is a female salmon, crab, or lobster. In Scotland hen is a term of endearment for a girl or woman. Of course a mother hen is very protective, while a hen with one chicken denotes a woman overly protective of her only child.

A hen party or hen night is an all-female get-together. The term eventually gave way to pajama party, but in Britain a hen night is also the distaff equivalent of a stag party, for a woman about to get married.

"As rare as hen's teeth" is extremely rare.

Hen money used to be money a woman got from selling spare eggs, then became a rather disparaging term for money women earned, somewhat equivalent to today's chump change (or chicken feed).

A hen harrier is a slender long-winged bird of prey of open country with nearly no resemblance to a hen. (The female is brown, the male mostly light gray.)

Hen and chickens is the name of a houseleek or other plant that yields small flower heads or offshoots. Henbit is a dead nettle with purple flowers whose 16th-century name is via Low German or Dutch meaning hen's bed—*hoenderbeet*. Henbane, as the name reveals, is poisonous, a member of the nightshade family, with sticky hairy leaves and an unpleasing aroma.

A henhouse is specially for hens, a place that needs guarding against hungry foxes. Symbolically, a henhouse is a place housing mostly or all females, such as a girls' dorm, that needs guarding against lustful males.

In English we say a chicken clucks—keeping in mind that most languages have different words for the way animals supposedly sound. When a person clucks, they're being fussy. When a person's a cluck, they're foolish, by association with a chicken. To emphasize this, one says someone is a dumb cluck.

Bill or Beak

When is it a bill and when a beak? Most ornithologists say they're one and the same but that the correct term is bill. Beak enters the non-technical picture when the bill is larger, as with parrots, toucans, flamingos, and pelicans. (Likewise, a person with a large honker is sometimes said to have quite a beak on him, not a bill.)

A bird's bony bill serves, depending, as its fork, knife, food processor, or serving dish. For instance, hummingbirds use their long slim bills to probe flowers for nectar, eagles' bills are hooked—the better to rip apart the flesh of their prey—and sparrows have tough conical bills for crushing seeds. In days of yore bills were considered avian noses, but they parallel mouths and jaws much more closely.

An old limerick says, "A wonderful bird is the pelican. Its beak can hold more than its belican."

(When humans bill and coo they speak or behave in a lovingly sentimental manner. A beaked whale has extended jaws that form a beak; among them are bottlenose whales.)

Cock and Bull Story

During the late 1700s and early 1800s Stony Stratford was a major stop-over site for mail coaches, tradesmen, and travelers, situated as it was halfway between London and Birmingham and halfway between Oxford and Cambridge. The town's two leading coaching inns were The Cock and The Bull, which became famous nationwide as the centers of almost all news and gossip traveling through either on foot or by horse. The rival inns began competing as to which could create the most exciting travelers' tales to pass on to the big cities. Too many of their stories were unbelievable and came to be known as cock and bull stories.

Cock

A cock is a rooster or male chicken—also a male lobster, crab, or salmon. Why did the word become "vulgar slang" (as dictionaries put it) for a penis? Theories abound. Because a cock was slang for an aggressive man. Because it was a fighting bird. Because a cock (the bird) has an upright posture—but so do umpteen animals, including kangaroos, often called roos in Australia. Because a rooster is a virile symbol—but so's a bull. Because a penis supposedly resembles a bird—a smaller one, not a male chicken. Because a man's pubic hair purportedly resembles the ring or collar of feathers displayed by some roosters and because the wattles on turkeys and some roosters are said to resemble the scrotum. Take your pick. Or come up with your own.

The word cock, for male bird, is of Germanic and Scandinavian origin.

Cockney

A Cockney is a London East Ender, traditionally born within the sound of Bow Bells. It's also that particular accent, once shunned by British media, now almost prized. In Australia it's a young snapper fish, and in the States it's someone who sounds like Michael Caine. Who would guess that the original meaning, in the 1300s, was a hen's egg? It was later used to describe a child breastfed for a longer than usual period, and then a pampered child. This led to signifying a feeble individual, which the country majority applied to the city minority, whose lifestyle they deemed less salutary than a rural one. All this by the 1600s, when

Cockney took on its current sense of describing a particular species of city dweller.

To Rule the Roost

The allusion is now to a rooster dominating the hens in a chicken run and trying to show his authority. Originally, the phrase had more to do with beef than poultry. Shakespeare helped popularize the phrase in his play *Henry VI Part II* (1591): "Suffolk, that new made man that rules the roast." This ties in with the "master" of the house carving and serving the roast meat. In 1637 Thomas Nabbes wrote in *Microcosmus*, "I am my lady's cook, and king of the kitchen where I rule the roast." In those days "roast" was pronounced with a long u-sound. In time, carving or ruling the roast metamorphosed into ruling the roost, with the same meaning.

To come home to roost means that something negative recoils upon the person responsible for it—fowl karma, say. E.g., "His misdeeds during his first term in office cost him being reelected."

A rooster tail is a spray of water thrown up behind a speedboat or surfboard, also a spray of gravel, dust, etc., thrown up behind a motor vehicle.

Cockatrice

This is a basilisk, a mythical reptile whose gaze or breath, take your pick, was lethal. It was hatched by a serpent from a cock's egg. The name is from the Greek *basiliskos*, little king, and was thus popular with nobles claiming royal descent in heraldry, where a cockatrice was often rendered as a two-legged dragon with a cock's head.

A basilisk is also a long Central American lizard—the male carries a crest running from head to tail. In olden days, crests and manes (usually male features) were viewed as symbols of royalty, power, and strength. Thus in various cultures the rooster was known as the little king of the barnyard.

Cock...

Several dog breeds are named after what they were intended to hunt or help hunt. One example is the cocker spaniel, whose ancestors were used to flush game birds like the woodcock from their cover.

Cockalorum is a dated term for an arrogant male, based on cock, as is the similar cock o' the walk. Cock-of-the-rock, however, is a tropical South American bird, a crested cotinga, the male of which sports bright red or orange plumage. (A major reason female birds are less colorfully eye-catching than males is their greater vulnerability to predators while sitting in the nest.)

Though cocky now denotes conceited, confident, or arrogant (as does cocksure), its 16th-century meaning was lecherous, via the horny rooster.

In Australia, cocky is the preferred term for cockatoo, a parrot with an erectile crest native to that land. Also native, crested, and related is the cockatiel, with a primarily gray body and orange and yellow face.

Some cocks have nothing to do with roosters. For instance a cock or small pile of hay may be of Scandinavian origin.

Cock- is a frequent prefix, not always fowl-related (e.g., cockroach is from the Spanish *cucaracha*, and cockamamie, now meaning ridiculous, had to do with decal-type designs).

Cocktails?

The origin of cocktail, the mixed drink, is vigorously disputed and varied. One theory: in the 1600s and 1700s beer was mixed with minced meat of boiled cock and other ingredients and named cock ale, which became cocktail. Another: trainers readying a rooster for a cock fight would feed their bird a combination of stale beer, white wine, gin, flour, seeds, and herbs. This was called cock-bread ale, later cock ale, later yet cocktail (and probably left the rooster cockeyed).

A third theory, from colonial America, involved tavern keepers, who stored alcohol in barrels. When almost empty, their dregs or tailings were combined in a single cask and sold at a lower price. That mixed alcohol, delivered through the cask's spigot or cock (now usually a stopcock), was cock tailings.

The first printed use of the word was in Britain in 1798 in *The Morning Post and Gazeteer*: "cock-tail (vulgarly called ginger)."

Cocktail can now mean a potent or dangerous mixture of things, as in a cocktail of prescription or illegal drugs.

(Cock-a-leekie is a traditional Scottish soup of chicken and leeks.)

Bird Mascots

Birds, all kinds of birds, have been used to advertise myriad products, including nightclubs (The Stork Club) and whiskey (Old Crow). In Mexico, the biggest tequila company is Cuervo (Crow), which this writer toured during one birthday in Tequila, a small town near Guadalajara.

Unusually, birds have been associated with shoe products, perhaps most famously Kiwi Shoe Polish (the small flightless New Zealand bird is its trademark), also Red Goose Shoes and Weatherbird Shoes (a rooster logo). Kiwi was the new name of the Chinese gooseberry, adopted in an advertising campaign that saw sales of the small green fruit soar.

Owls have been associated with wisdom since ancient Greece, where an owl was the mascot of the goddess Athena, after whom Athens was named. Thus they're often associated with "smart" products or nighttime ones. Montgomery Ward used the Wise-Buy Owl to sell its Riverside tires—the owl sported a service station attendant's cap and carried a tire beneath one wing, but also wore glasses. Owl Drugs was a major drugstore chain and Sanborn's, the Mexican gift shop/restaurant chain (owned by reportedly the richest man in the world), uses three owls perched on a branch with a crescent moon behind them as its logo.

Penguins seem to wear tuxedoes, and many tux-rental shops use them as mascots. Munsingwear Clothing uses a penguin to advertise its sharp clothing line. In 1935, an English publisher launched Penguin Books, intended as the first paperback line of quality books, as opposed to pulp fiction. (There was already an Albatross Book Company.) Willie the penguin was the cute front for Brown & Williamson Tobacco's heavily mentholated Kool cigarettes. When the corporation brought out salt and pepper shakers, they introduced Willie's mate Millie. Early on, Swanson, who developed frozen TV dinners, used a penguin logo.

During the late 1950s and into the '60s, the best known chicken mascot was that which sat atop Chicken Delight eateries. He wore a chef's toque and with one wing held aloft a plate of biscuits. The nationally famous slogan was "Don't cook tonight, call Chicken Delight!" The company eventually went under due to management problems and competition from what's now called KFC. (Whenever chickens are used to advertise fried chicken, they're alive and smiling or laughing, before the fact.)

Varig the Brazilian airline boasted a big-billed toucan-like bird in sunglasses and hat, ready for the beaches of Rio de Janeiro. Two of the better-known cereal mascots were the multicolored Fruit Loops toucan and Sonny the Cuckoo Bird who's manically "cuckoo for Cocoa Puffs!"

A briefly successful mascot of the late '50s was Fresh-Up Freddie, an energetic rooster created to sell Seven-Up. He ran around singing, "Nothing does it like Seven-Up, Seven-Up! Ooo-oo! Ooo-oo! Nothing does it like Seven-Up!" However, in each ad Freddie wore a different hat and seemed to display a different personality. The only consistency was his mania for that particular soft drink. Much longer-lasting is the green and red rooster on packages of Kellogg's Corn Flakes. Cornelius, a.k.a. Corny, likewise bowed in the late '50s. He was chosen because a rooster reportedly signified getting the morning off to a good start—as would a bowl of Corny's cereal.

Flamingo

The name of this unique pink or scarlet bird goes back to the 16th century and *flamengo* in Spanish, an earlier form of flamenco, Spain's unique style of guitar music and dance whose female performers often wore red. The word also meant Fleming, a Flemish-speaking native of Belgium, once part of the Netherlands, which Spain ruled for a time, and is related to the Latin *flamma*, flame, as in flame-red.

Flamenco was first applied to Gypsy dancing in southern Spain's Andalusia. A peacock seems more apt for describing the proud, chest-forward (for both genders), self-consciously showy style of flamenco dance than a flamingo, which, when not simply standing on one leg, often has its head in the water, feeding. (Although flamingos' knees look like they bend backwards, they don't—those are their ankles; the knees are higher up, hidden by plumage. Penguins also have hidden knees.)

A gypsy moth is a woodland moth the male of which is brown and the female of which is white and larger but cannot fly. For short distances she can latch on to a traveler. For longer ones, she crawls up a tree and lets the wind carry her.

(Gypsies were misnamed in English, for they didn't originate in Egypt, but in India.)

To Sing Like a Canary

Although to "sing like a canary" is a compliment, non-musically it means betrayal, though betrayal of a (usually fellow) criminal or criminal activity. Since the 1920s canary has been slang for a police informer, while singing has signified betrayal since the 1500s or before. In his 1815 novel *Guy Mannering* Sir Walter Scott wrote, "To sing out or whistle in the cage, is when a rogue, being apprehended, peaches against his comrades." The latter verb meant to tattle. "Tattle" in the UK was idle talk or gossip, but in North America it came to mean reporting wrongdoing.

Gangster movies of the 1930s popularized both "singing" and "canary" in reference to crooks selling each other out for preferential treatment from the law or a reduced sentence. A 1984 *New York Post* headline blared, "Mob Canary Sings Again for the Feds."

An avian canary is a melodious, bright yellow finch—often kept in a cage.

A canary creeper is a South American climbing plant that produces bright yellow flowers, while canary grass is grown for its seeds, which are fed to cage birds.

P.S. The Canary Islands weren't named after the bird. The name derives from dogs the Romans saw on what they called the *Canariae Insulae*, islands of the dogs. Most sources say they weren't dogs, but seals, which doesn't say much for the Romans' eyesight. The birds from the islands were then named canaries—after the alleged dogs. Woof!

Stool Pigeon

North America once numbered billions of passenger pigeons, which the British colonists extensively hunted for food. They became extinct in the early 20th century. Passenger pigeons were often attached by string to "stools"—perches—as hunters' decoys (stool is related to the obsolete stall, meaning a decoy).

The first use of stool pigeon relating to humans involved decoys employed to entice passersby into a betting game. By the mid 1800s the phrase took on its current meaning of police informer, as in an 1849 issue of *Banker's Magazine* which reported that a senior Philadelphia constable had used a particular individual "as a 'stool pigeon' or secret informer." In the next century, stool pigeon and canary became practically synonymous.

An alternate meaning of "stool-pigeoning" was provided in Bartlett's 1848 *Dictionary of Americanisms*, stating that police "of olden times" would often arrest someone they deemed a shady character, then demand money or jewelry in exchange for his freedom. In other words, blackmail. Sometimes the character was indeed shady and had no money or valuables but instead traded information for his release.

Urban pigeons are often missing toes. The reasons include land-based predators (meow…) which attack roosting pigeons, fungal infections from the dirty locales pigeons often frequent, and avian pox that can shrivel their toes until they fall off. Also, accidents occur when pigeons' feet get caught in cracks or crevices or while flying they collide with TV antennae and utility wires.

Ugly Duckling

Ugly duckling is a misnomer—baby ducks are beautiful as well as adorable. That a duckling can grow up to be a swan is an impossibility. The concept of plainness eventually blossoming into beauty is plausible, but its most famous version, Hans Christian Andersen's fairy tale, relies on mistaken identity. A swan's egg is mistakenly hatched among a duck's eggs. Mama duck tries to protect her presumed boy-chick from criticism and abuse, but the misfit cygnet is made to feel unattractive and ashamed, and hides himself away. Come spring-time, he turns into a swan, more beautiful—and far taller—than his former fellow ducks.

Psychologist Dr. Betty Berzon cites "Two points. The unwarranted labeling of a given animal as 'ugly,' plus unrealistic expectations. Not all so-called ugly ducklings grow into swans. Some become attractive ducks, some merely become less plain. The most valid conclusions here are focusing less on looks, more on self-worth, and treating everybody well."

Swan...

A swansong is the final creation, performance, or activity of a person's career, especially an artist's. According to legend, a swan sings but once, when about to die. The 19th-century term is from the German *Schwanengesang*, a mythical song sung by a dying swan. (The most famous ballet is Tchai-kovsky's *Swan Lake*.)

The expression "all your swans are geese" means all one's hopes have been disappointed—the concept being swans' superiority to geese. By contrast, all your geese are swans implies that someone overvalues their possessions just because they belong to them.

To swan is British slang for moving or walking in an ostentatious or a casual or irresponsible way.

A swan dive is US slang for a shallow dive.

A swan mussel is a big mussel whose larvae parasitize fish.

A swan neck is a curved structure with the shape of a swan's neck (similar to gooseneck).

Swansdown is used for trimmings and powder puffs. It's also a thick cotton fabric with a soft nap on one side or a soft, thick woolen fabric containing some silk or cotton.

Swan-upping is the annual catching of swans on the River Thames in England to mark them to show ownership by a corporation or the Crown.

A Lame Duck and a Quack

A lame duck is someone unable to fend for themselves—like, literally, a lame duck—but is most often used in the phrase a lame-duck president, one whose term of office is nearly at an end, likewise his influence, and/or a second-term president whose patronage has diminished and who is less effective legislatively.

The first people called lame ducks were 17th-century members of the London Stock Exchange who couldn't pay their debts and so lost their seats and reputations. By the early 1860s, American officeholders were also lame ducks, especially holdover congressmen, possibly thanks to the hunter's maxim "Never waste powder on a dead duck."

Quack, the derogatory word for doctor, has nothing to do with ducks. This word is short for quacksalver, a 16th-century sobriquet for one who sold fraudulent medicines. (As did the second wave of snake-oil salesmen in the 19th century—see an upcoming entry.) Quack meant to peddle; salver is from a salve or ointment. Today a quack is a real doctor, but an inept and/or unethical one.

Duck...

The word duck evolved from a Germanic root meaning a diving bird. As with goose, the basic word also denotes the female of the species, with drake (like gander) signifying the male. As a favorite game bird, ducks were much on humans' minds, as mirrored in the myriad of duck words, names, and phrases.

A duck is also a white thin-shelled bivalve mollusk found on the American Atlantic coast. In cricket a duck is a batsman's score of zero, short for duck's egg, meaning the figure 0.

Duck, the strong fabric used for work clothes and sails, isn't from the bird, but a Dutch word for linen. Likewise, ducks—trousers made from duck.

Ducks is an informal British term of endearment: "'allo, ducks," sometimes ducky. (In the US ducky means delightful, often sarcastically: "Isn't that just ducky.")

To duck is to quickly lower the head or body, usually for defensive purposes.

To duck something is to evade or avoid it. The verb also means to avoid playing a winning card on a particular trick for tactical reasons in bridge. Or to push someone under water.

A ducking stool was used in olden times to punish someone, plunging them into a river or pond in a chair attached to the end of a pole (an example of "cruel and unusual punishment" obviated by the US Constitution).

Duckboards are wooden planks joined together to make a path over muddy ground.

Duck mussels are found in rivers with sandy or gravelly beds, while duckweed is a minute flowering plant found in profusion upon still water.

Ducks and drakes is a game of throwing a flat stone along the water's surface and counting how many times it bounces on the water.

To play ducks and drakes is to not take something very seriously.

A duckpin is a short, squat bowling pin. To duckwalk is to walk while squatting.

Duck soup is US slang for an easy task, also the name of a classic Marx Brothers movie.

Duck's ass is the nickname of a male hairdo slicked back at the sides and tapered upwards at the end to resemble a duck's derriere.

An odd or queer duck (or bird) is a person adjudged as peculiar.

To be a dead duck (or pigeon) is to have failed, sometimes ominously. A dead duck is a cause or campaign without relevance to modern life.

To be a sitting duck is to be readily exploited or exposed (like the duck figures in a shooting gallery), from the notion that it's easy to shoot a duck that's sitting still.

Like water off a duck's back implies criticism or advice that has no effect.

To get or have one's ducks in a row is US slang for getting or having everything organized.

To take to something like a duck to water is to take to something very readily.

Two shakes of a duck's tail means very quickly or very soon—"two seconds" on telephone-hold typically means two minutes.

Fine day for ducks is said when it's raining.

Fair Game

Today anyone or anything can be fair game according to someone else's estimation or justification, but originally fair game referred to part of 32 hunting laws introduced in the

18th century by George III (the king who lost the American colonies and went mad). The laws were an effort to reduce poaching and protect landowners—in other words, the rich, including himself—from theft of livestock. Historian Albert Jack explained, "The idea was to keep hunting the privilege of the aristocracy, but was cloaked in the notion that without controls game stock would be severely depleted."

By the early 1800s it was illegal for anybody to remove game from any land except the squire and his eldest son. To steal even one pheasant could result in being transported for seven years to Australia (then a penal colony at the end of the world). The only exceptions were a few small birds and vermin—wild mammals and birds harmful to the landowners' crops. Those were "fair game."

Eating Crow

Farmers long had reason to hate crows, the bold black birds which, if not scared off from newly seeded wheat fields or spring cornfields, would rip the plants out of the ground, eat the seeds or kernels, and so slash a farmer's yield. Thus, some farmers facing an unpleasant outcome or the humiliation of defeat would declare it was like having to eat crow.

A popular legend about the phrase's origin tells of a soldier who went hunting and accidentally shot a tame crow. Along came its owner, who grabbed the soldier's gun and ordered, "Eat crow or die." After the soldier had eaten half the bird—raw?—the owner told him he could stop. At that point the soldier regained his gun, turned it on the other man, and ordered, "Now *you* eat crow or die."

Those who have eaten crow say it tastes like most game birds.

"Eating boiled crow," as the saying originally went, was most widespread in the 19th century as a reference to publicly humiliated politicians. Men running for and already in office were typically more affluent than average folk, who often had to hunt their own food. Due to its color and scavenger status, crow was considered a meal of desperation. By century's end, the symbolic "eating crow" rarely included "boiled" and lost its political connotation, simply indicating that someone in the wrong had to apologize.

One Fell Swoop

Fell means terrible or ferocious and is related to the word felon. Fell also meant an animal's skin or hide with its fur. The phrase in or at one fell swoop connotes a bird of prey scooping up one or more victims at a single go and was made famous in Shakespeare's *Macbeth* (published 1623). When Macduff finds out his children and wife have all been killed, he howls, "What, all my pretty chickens, and their dam, at one fell swoop?"

Dam is the female parent of an animal, especially a mammal. It's related to *dame*, French for lady (as in madame, my lady), corrupted in American English into dame, a non-complimentary word for woman.

Dodo

"Dead as a dodo" used to be a more common expression than it is now, and unlike today's "dead as a doornail" wasn't just alliterative. Dodos, found on the Indian Ocean island of Mauritius, were bulky flightless birds that survived through eons because their habitat included no predators. Then came Europeans, specifically, Portuguese—who, also in the Indian Ocean, tried but failed to obliterate Buddhism from Ceylon (now Sri Lanka). They named the bird *doudo*, Portuguese for stupid, because the running birds couldn't escape them.

The Europeans brought pigs to the island (and, accidentally, rats), which ran wild and destroyed the dodos' nests, eggs, and young. By the late 1600s dodos, targeted by the three newcomer species, had become extinct, one of the first recorded species to suffer that sadly accelerating fate.

In English, partly because of its funny sound and the "stupid" image (bolstered by extinction), dumb as a dodo became an emphatic equivalent for stupid, later shortening to just dodo. The most famous illustration of a dodo is Tenniel's in *Alice's Adventures in Wonderland*.

Snipe and Shrike

A snipe is a not very pleasant wading bird with a long straight bill that it uses to attack other birds and even loudspeakers. It's very sensitive to sound, including a rival's mating call, which impels it to dive through the air, its wing feathers vibrating in anger. Hence, it's the origin of to snipe at someone (as in a verbal attack) and sniper.

A snipe eel is a slender eel with a long, thin beak-like snout, while a snipefish has a long, slender snout with its mouth at the tip. Again, aquatic creatures are frequently compared to and named after more familiar land or avian animals.

A shrike is a predatory songbird with a hooked bill it uses to impale victims, often onto thorns. *The Shrike*, a 1955 movie, concerned a wife, improbably played by screen sweetheart June Allyson, who had her husband committed; her actions were likened to the destructive bird's.

To Go Belly-Up

Children with pet goldfish—an animal one can't pet (the Spanish for a pet is *mascota*)—learn some hard life lessons from their fishbowl or aquarium denizens. There's the shock of finding a fish missing, with the realization that a bigger, stronger fish has devoured a companion. Also the sadness and objectification of death, when one sees a goldfish floating belly-up, due to the gas that fills its stomach as it decays, causing the body to flip over, with the weightier backboned half below and the lighter gas-filled belly above.

Ergo, to go belly-up, which besides meaning to die came to symbolize bankruptcy. It also evolved into a verb with separate meanings, as in a saloon that went belly-up and had to be sold or to belly-up to the bar for a drink.

Drinking Like a Fish

Because many fish swim open-mouthed, some people got the idea they were constantly drinking water. Hence, to drink like a fish came to refer to alcoholic humans. Fish sometimes drink water accidentally, when they eat (so do some alcoholics).

What has a group of fish to do with school? Nothing, though a group of fish is called a school or a shoal of fish. Both derive from the Dutch root *schole*, meaning a crowd or troop. How educational.

Fishy Expressions

Fish usually smell fishy. Not a judgment. In a non-culinary context, fishy is a judgment, a negative one. Interesting that fish is the sole flesh whose natural taste and/or smell chefs and cooks often disguise or neutralize, for example, via sauces, a given preparation, or just sprinkling on lemon juice.

To fish in troubled or muddy waters is to take advantage of a troubled or confused situation. To feed the fishes has two meanings: to be seasick, to drown.

It's a rare person who doesn't sometimes fish for information or compliments—possibly a cold fish. Such people may only care what they think and have other or bigger fish to fry. Or figure there are plenty of other fish in the ocean.

Fish or cut bait is an order to make up your mind and do it—stop wasting time or let someone else have a turn.

"That has nothing to do with the price of fish" means that something is irrelevant.

A fish story is one told by a fisherman, usually exaggerated, often fishy. A fish tale may be an exaggerated or woeful story, as in: "You don't believe her fish tale, do you?"

A whale isn't a fish, but a mammal—yet how often does one see its hair? The phrase "a whale of a good time" simply reflects the whale's size; the Blue Whale is the largest creature that ever lived, including the dinosaurs.

Little Fish, Big Fish

Sometimes people have to decide whether they want to be a big fish in a small pond or a small fish in a big pond. Some who choose the latter find that they feel like a fish out of water. Some people are content to be small fry. Some who become a big fish in a big pond find they're living life in a goldfish bowl. And some people are happy within themselves and need something else like a fish needs a bicycle—or as feminist Gloria Steinem put it, "A woman without a man is like a fish without a bicycle."

Ever wondered why little fish in large aquariums aren't scared stiff whenever big fish, like sharks, approach? Basically because as long as the big fish are well fed, they won't bother with the small fry. Also, little fish are agile snacks—not a meal—and may not be worth a big fish's time and bother. It's unknown how, but fish can tell when a predator fish becomes hungry, and as soon as they get the signal, they can disappear, especially in an aquarium, where they have reef structure, etc., to dive into or behind. Plus, in the confines of a space smaller than the sea, a little fish can typically outmaneuver a big fish. So there.

Fish Terms

There are far more creatures in the sea than just fish, but fish being the standard for humans—the one caught and eaten most often—their name is used in those of invertebrates that also dwell underwater. For instance, shellfish, jellyfish, and starfish. The Olde English word *fisc* was originally used for any animal living in water.

Even underwater there are creatures named lice—the fish louse is a parasitic crustacean that attaches itself to piscine gills or skin.

A fish eagle is a rare eagle that lives primarily on fish. A fish hawk is an osprey, a big fish-eating bird of prey whose name comes from Latin words meaning bone (*os*) and to break—the bird has a powerful beak.

What are edible fish fingers in the United Kingdom are usually called fish sticks in the United States.

Originally a fishwife was a woman who sold fish. To sell them, she had to hawk them, or yell out her sales pitch. In time, fishwife came to mean an ill-mannered or low-class female prone to shouting. (Who nowadays might wear fishnet stockings?)

An old trout is, per the dictionary, an annoying or bad-tempered old woman. To play someone like a trout is similar to playing the fish one hopes to catch, alternating slack, heavy, and light pressure in order to land it. E.g., "The blonde starlet played the elderly millionaire like a trout."

A silverfish is a grayish bristletail insect, so named because of its color and undulating, fishlike movement. Its scientific name, *Lepisma saccharina*, indicates its preferred diet of sugars and starches.

When an automobile fishtails, its rear moves uncontrollably sideways.

A fisheye lens has a wide angle, up to 180 degrees, the scale (no pun) reduced toward the edges. To give someone the fisheye is an American expression for looking at them in an unfriendly or suspicious manner.

Unrelated to any sea creature are fish and fishplate, which are metal or wooden pieces used to strengthen or fix joints, masts, rails, and masonry—their common name is from a French word meaning to fix and going back of course to Latin.

Fish in Latin is *piscis*, plural *pisces*, the name of the large constellation Fish or Fishes, representing two fish tied together by their tails. Pisces is the twelfth and final sign of the zodiac.

A Pretty Kettle of Fish

A pretty kettle of fish is a predicament with no easy solution. When Queen Mary found out her son Edward VIII had to choose between marrying two-time American divorcee Wallis Simpson and giving up the throne, she declared, "This is a pretty kettle of fish!"

Picnics in 18th-century Scotland began with the annual salmon run and were held on river banks. The fish were cooked in big kettles and were eaten with the fingers. Not a pretty sight, and the adjective preceding kettle of fish was intended ironically, as with a now almost obsolete American phrase, a pretty picnic.

The phrase a different kettle of fish is akin to a horse of another color.

Natural Coloring

A very few animals gave their names to colors. Including coral, which are the external skeletons of colonial marine creatures that form reefs. The color is a pinkish red, though coral comes in various shades. Coral also means the edible unfertilized roe of a lobster or scallop that reddens when cooked.

Salmon is also a color, pinkish orange. A salmonberry is a North American bramble with an edible pink raspberry-like fruit. The name of gravlax, the Scandinavian dish of dry-cured salmon marinated in herbs, comes from *grav*, trench, and *lax*, salmon, as the fish used to be buried in salt in a hole in the ground.

Salmonella is not named after the fish, but after Dr. Daniel Salmon—maybe his paternal ancestors were named after the fish—who was a veterinary surgeon (1850–1914).

Caviar, Clams, and Oysters

Caviar is, but of course, the pickled roe of sturgeon or other big fish, and very expensive, unless it comes from, say, lumpfish. The phrase caviar for the general means something of quality that is wasted on the uncultivated. It doesn't imply that military generals have no taste (this writer's maternal grandfather was a general; no idea if he liked caviar). It's yet another expression whose tail got chopped off: general *public*…. Shakespeare used it in *Hamlet* (1603): "The play, I remember, pleased not the million; 'twas caviare to the general." When caviar was introduced to England in the late 1500s it took time for the public—those who could afford it—to get used to it.

Another abbreviated expression, a rude way of saying be quiet, was originally shut your clam-trap. Not the final but the penultimate word got dropped—shut your trap. Someone who does is said to clam up or to close up like a clam. As for happy as a clam, it's been suggested that an open clam gives the appearance of smiling. The expression was originally happy as a clam at high water.

Clam is one of many slang words for a dollar. It too was shortened, from clamshell—several Native American tribes, especially in California, used clamshells as currency.

If the world is one's oyster, one has abundant opportunities and a bright future. In *The Merry Wives of Windsor* (1602) Shakespeare wrote, "Why, then, the world is mine oyster, which I with sword will open." Anticipating of course a pearl. To be as close as an oyster is to be secretive, imparting little or no information.

Holy Mackerel...

Of numerous exclamations beginning with holy, "holy mackerel" was among the most widespread. The fish, among the cheapest, was one of the most popular. In 19th-century North America Protestants sometimes nicknamed Catholic immigrants mackerel-snappers, both because the fish was more common among poor people and their mandated eating of fish on Fridays. Later, the nickname shortened to mackerels.

Holy mackerel was first recorded in 1803, but the exclamation was in use since the 1600s because in some places mackerel was allowed to be sold on Sundays—the "holy day" (related to holiday)—since its quality deteriorated fast. So mackerel was a "holy fish." The expression's acme of popularity was the late 1920s via radio's long-running #1 hit show *Amos 'n' Andy*, a comedy with two white men impersonating two black men. (The #2 show made more sense: Jewish actor-writer-producer Gertrude Berg starred as Molly Goldberg in *The Goldbergs*.)

Dead as a mackerel seems to have developed out of the 16th-century phrase mute as a fish, meaning silent. Alliteration and specificity changed the phrase to mute as a mackerel. Another contemporary expression was dead as a herring, which reportedly came under the influence of mute as a mackerel and emerged dead as a mackerel—and has stayed that way.

A mackerel shark is a porbeagle, a big, energetic shark encountered in the North Atlantic and Mediterranean. Its unlikely name is probably from the Cornish porth, harbor or cove, and bugel, shepherd.

A mackerel sky is the same as a buttermilk sky, covered with altocumulus clouds that give a patterned, scalelike appearance.

To throw a sprat to catch a mackerel signifies investing a minor sum in hopes of making a major profit.

Red Herring

Herring was one of the fish most frequently extracted from British coastal waters in the 18th and 19th centuries.

Pre-refrigeration, it was very practical when preserved via a salting and smoking process that made it a deep brownish-red. The reason red herring came to mean a false clue—as in murder mystery novels and Hitchcock movies—was its use as a false scent starting in the early 1800s, when many a fox's life was spared by individual Brits who didn't hold with the then-custom of blood sports. On hunt days these pioneering animal activists and/or opponents of the class system would drag the pungent-smelling preserved fish across the path of the hunt and away from the fox, thereby deceiving the aristocrats' dogs, who followed the stronger scent—a red herring.

A now almost obsolete expression is "neither fish, flesh, fowl, nor good red herring." In *King Henry IV, Part I* (1598) Shakespeare had Falstaff say of an otter, "Why, she's neither fish nor flesh, a man knows not where to have her." The complete expression meant something was neither this nor that and thus satisfied nobody. It reflected the strict dietary laws of the Catholic Church centuries ago. Monks were forbidden to eat fish, most people weren't allowed to eat flesh—meat—and the poor were forbidden red herring. (Well, there are plenty more fish in the sea.)

Hook, Line, and Sinker

Being extremely gullible is to swallow something hook, line, and sinker, in the same way that a hungry, gullible fish swallows not just a baited hook but the lead weight—a sinker—and some of the line.

FYI and anyone else's, not long ago, a young Australian proved, reportedly for the first time, that fish do feel pain when they're caught.

Like Sardines

Fact: there is no such fish as a sardine. Sardine is a generic marketing term. What it comprises varies from country to country—in Norway sprat and immature herring, in Portugal and France young pilchards, in the US sprats, small herring, brisling, and pilchards (by law, not anchovies). Before World War I sardines were typically used for fish meal. During the Great Depression they became very popular as an inexpensive and nutritious snack or meal. Sales since WWII haven't matched the pre-war numbers.

The US sardine industry has always been based in Maine and California.

The word sardine was first recorded in the 15th century, from the Italian island of Sardinia, around which many little fish were caught.

As an experiment, ask to buy fresh sardines at a fish market—see the reactions and whether anybody explains that they only come, packed, in cans.

Lobster...

The rich used to look down their noses at lobster as food for the poor. Readily available on the American east coast, the sea product was inexpensive before it became in demand by the cognoscenti (remember when chicken wings were practically given away?). It began changing with the famed Delmonico's restaurant and its cayenne-flavored Lobster à la Wenberg, introduced to the New York eatery by ship owner Ben Wenberg. After he and Lorenz Delmonico had a bitter falling out, the restaurant substituted Lobster à la Delmonico, but it didn't catch on. Diners demanded the return of the original dish, so the stubborn Delmonico reluctantly reinstated it, but switched two of the letters (plus one), renaming it Lobster Newburg.

Interestingly, lobster comes from Latin *locusta*, meaning locust or crustacean.

A lobster moth is brown and is so named because its caterpillar has an upturned tail resembling a lobster's.

A lobster pot is a basket-like trap in which to catch lobsters. Betty White has stated, "It's one thing to eat a lobster, another to boil it while alive. Inhumane and gourmet really shouldn't be compatible words."

Octopus

When humans first saw octopi they probably thought how much grasping eight arms could do. The innocent octopus has since symbolized grasping and greed. In Central America, for instance, the United Fruit Company, which had its own army, was known as *el pulpo*, the octopus (at the American company's behest President Eisenhower okayed an invasion of Guatemala in 1954).

An octopus is soft-bodied, with no interior shell but tough beak-like jaws. Technically its plural, being a Greek name, is octopodes, though the Latin-patterned octopi is traditionally used. However, most people who say it at all say octopuses.

Octopussy was the title of a James Bond movie based on an Ian Fleming short story and an octoroon is someone who's one-eighth black (the term is now archaic).

Crab...

In 1300s coastal England crabbed meant grouchy, as from a painful nip via a crab's claws. Crabby developed separately in the late 1700s from Olde English crabba, via a Germanic root meaning to scratch or claw.

Crabs, or crab lice, would make anyone crabby (see Lice, further on), as would walking crabwise, or sideways.

A crab apple is small and sour, and a crab spider has long front legs that move sidewise.

Crab grass is a hard-to-get-rid-of creeping warm-weather plant also known as summer grass, fall grass, and finger grass. It originated in Oriental tropics and by the 1600s was a thriving marine grass in salt marshes of the US South. Its name was crop grass, but as with many other words the p elided into a b, softening the o into an a. Some say American slaves effected the pronunciation change. Also, some say that the flat spreading mat of crab grass with three-pronged seed heads resembles a crab. (Some imagination.)

Shrimp

In the United States, both a small and a larger edible crustacean with ten legs is a shrimp. In the United Kingdom, the bigger one is called a prawn to avoid confusion. (Jumbo shrimp, often advertised in American buffets, is an oxymoron.) Shrimp comes from an old Germanic word meaning to contract or grow smaller, which probably led to its use as a name for the small crustacean and, later, a small or puny person. (Because human toes somewhat resemble shrimp, shrimping now means, besides catching shrimp, sucking toes for sexual stimulation.)

What the US calls a shrimp cocktail is in Britain a prawn cocktail. Describing the appetizer as a cocktail came about during Prohibition, when America unrealistically banned alcohol. Thus, in the 1920s it became fashionably impudent to order a shrimp (or fruit) "cocktail."

A shrimp plant is a Mexican shrub so named because its clusters of small pink-brown flowers somewhat resemble shrimp.

Cockles

Warming the cockles of one's heart is redundant and a misnomer. Cockles are edible burrowing bivalve mollusks (tasty, no?). They were once a dietary staple for people in coastal Britain and Ireland. The mythic Molly Malone pushed her wheelbarrow through Dublin's fair city crying, "Cockles and mussels, alive, alive-o!" Cockles were deemed to resemble a heart, but a human heart, not a Valentine heart.

In medieval Latin the heart's ventricles were *cochleae cordis*, which may have led surgeons to refer to those particular mollusks as cochleae, mispronouncing the word (which means snails) and adding an s. Most people either esteemed or reviled doctors, whose primary medical practice—and they needed practice—was bleeding people (the main cause of George Washington's death after contracting a common cold), whether or not the patient needed it. Patients of yore had to be very patient, which might seem the origin of a "patient," but that's from the Latin meaning to suffer. Surgeons, unlike doctors, were mostly looked up to, and their word usage sometimes filtered through to the masses.

So warming the cockles of one's heart is like saying warming the hearts of one's heart, and literally means warming the snails of one's heart. The Latin for a snail is *cochlea*, the modern anatomic name of the human inner ear, with its snail-like construction.

Apropos of snails, did you know the average Frenchperson eats about ten *escargots* a year?

Sea Stars, Not Starfish

Starfish is an obvious misnomer, and experts, even ichthyologists (who study fish), call them sea stars. They're categorized as *Echinodermata* (spiny-skinned) and despite appearances are aggressive carnivores who spend most of their time trawling for food. They are deaf and don't have eyes but do have an eyehole on each arm or leg—take your pick—which senses light. The groove beneath each (let's say) leg is lined with hundreds of teeny tube feet that propel sea stars and are suction cups, besides. Although sea stars don't have noses—or faces, for that matter—they've a good sense of smell which aids in detecting prey. Sea stars do have mouths, right under their centers. Their favorite meals include oysters, mussels, and clams, also fish and coral.

Prying open an oyster isn't easy for a human, but a sea star wraps its legs or arms around it and uses its tube feet to force a crack—one one-hundredth of an inch will do—at which point the sea star protrudes its stomach into the oyster shell, its digestive juices helping to digest the oyster. It may take 24 hours to fully digest its prey, at which satiated stage the sea star retracts its stomach and puts it back inside its own mouth. (No wonder they don't dare show their non-faces.)

Jumping the Shark

Because it's so relatively recent, this phrase's origin can be attributed exactly. The website www.jumptheshark.com went online on December 24, 1997. Devoted to critiques of TV shows, it defined jumping the shark as the point "when you know that your favorite television program has reached its peak ... from now on ... it's all downhill." This subjective appraisal may be caused by a series marrying off its central character or making her pregnant, replacing an actor with another (as in *Bewitched* and *Charlie's Angels*), killing off a character (as in soap operas galore), or too many guest stars (trying to make up for weak plots).

In the case of *Happy Days*, which debuted in 1974, the come-down was a stunt. The character of Fonzie (Henry Winkler), whose popularity grew to surpass that of series star Ron Howard as Richie Cunningham, went waterskiing in trunks and his signature leather jacket and ... jumped over a shark. That outlandish episode caused many viewers to henceforth take the show even less seriously.

On the other hand, that episode aired in 1977 and *Happy Days* continued for another seven years. Site founder Jon Hein credited his roommate with coining the expression, which now applies not only to TV shows, but anything or anyone in public life, including politicians.

Loan Shark

This bit of US slang dates back to the 1860s but was commonly known by the early 1900s as a modern term for usurer—usury was outlawed in 1917. Of course many or most loan sharks operated, and still do, outside the law. Professor Rosemarie Ostler notes that "Along with the bears and bulls of the stock market, the loan shark was a force to be reckoned with. Like many business titans, he would do whatever it took to make a profit." Three reasons for the term: a) both types of shark are predatory, b) the tighter and tighter circles both types make around their prey, and c) as a shark's bite is often lethal, so the revenge of the human type that isn't repaid.

Through the 1950s and into the '70s, many TV programs wouldn't allow a character to say "loan shark" lest it offend savings-and-loan advertisers.

Shark…

Though shark itself is of unknown origin, phrases derived from it are clear and mostly negative. A human shark is someone who swindles others, usually in specific fields, for example, a pool shark or card shark. In Britain shark practice (sometimes sharp practice) means dishonesty in business or gambling.

A shark is also a grayish brown moth.

Sharkskin is a once-fashionable, somewhat shiny, rather stiff fabric. One devotee of sharkskin suits was singer Bobby Darin, whose hit "Mack the Knife" starts, "Oh, the shark has pretty teeth, dear…."

To "miss the sharks while netting the minnows" translates to succeeding at little things while failing in bigger ones.

Swimming with sharks, typically in a business context, is something that—as the movie of the same name confirms—not everyone survives.

> ## Charlie the Tuna
>
> One of the longest-running commercial animal mascots was Charlie the Tuna, for StarKist Tuna. The ads were meant to emphasize the company's insistence on good-tasting tuna. Charlie would read a classic novel, say, to prove to StarKist that he had good taste. The rejoinder was always, "Sorry, Charlie, StarKist doesn't want tuna with good taste, StarKist wants tuna that tastes good." (Why Charlie wished to volunteer himself to be gutted, sliced, cooked, and canned was never explained.)

A Frog in One's Throat

Medieval belief held that it was possible to swallow frogspawn while drinking from a stream or pond—this, before modern drinking water—and therefore tadpoles could hatch inside a person's stomach. They would try to escape upwards, making it difficult for the afflicted host to speak with a frog in one's throat.

Medieval doctors sometimes prescribed putting a frog inside one's mouth against infections like the fungus called thrush (also the name of a chronic condition afflicting the frog of a horse's foot—see next entry). They believed the frog's head, as it breathed inside a human's mouth, would absorb the infection into itself. (Quack-quack.)

It can't really rain cats and dogs, but it occasionally rains frogs, fish, or soda cans. Violent thunderstorms and tornadoes may suck up all the contents of a small pond and carry them aloft until they're dropped back to earth. In 1883 in Cairo, Illinois, a heavy rain brought down hundreds if not thousands of one-inch frogs. "A shower of frogs" had blanketed Kansas City, Missouri, in 1873, and in 1995 a tornado ripped through a Midwestern bottling plant, eventually depositing soda cans 150 miles north of the plant. A witness reported, "Soda cans were falling from the sky just like raining frogs."

Frogs

In the 1700s frog became an English nickname for the French, via alliteration (both words begin with fr-) and that nationality's consumption of frog legs.

Other uses of frog, often as a prefix, are harder to explain. For instance, a frog is an ornamental fastener often seen in Western versions of Chinese clothes comprising a spindle-shaped button that fits in a loop. Or the frog that's a horny elastic pad growing in the sole of a horse's hoof that helps it absorb the shock when its hoof hits the ground.

Then there's the frog that's a spiky or perforated object, usually in the bottom of a vase, used to hold the stems of flowers in an arrangement. And the frog that is or was a belt attachment to hold a sword or bayonet.

To frogmarch someone is to force them to walk ahead by pinning or holding their arms from behind. More logically, a frogman is a diver wearing a wetsuit and flippers, with breathing equipment for working underwater.

Frogbit is a freshwater floating plant with bunches of small rounded leaves.

A frogmouth is a nocturnal bird from Southeast Asia and Australia that resembles a nightjar. Frogfish are anglerfish that dwell on the seabed, their bumpy complexions serving as camouflage. A froghopper is a plant-sucking bug that hops from site to site, leaving behind its frothy white larvae on leaves and plant stems—these deposits are known as cuckoo spit (crazy, huh?).

FYI, frogs cannot swallow unless they close their eyes. That's because their eyes bulge not only outward but inward, so their eyes have to help push food into their stomachs—something humans do with their tongues. Frogs also must depress their eyes in order to breathe, since they lack a diaphragm.

Toads

To call a person a toad is one of the lowest animal comparisons. It means they're really repulsive, physically or morally.

A toady is an apple-polisher or, vulgarly, a kiss-ass. The verb to toady, or behave obsequiously, is a 19th-century contraction of toad-eater, an assistant to a snake-oil salesman who was willing to eat toads—regarded as poisonous—to prove that the snake oil worked.

The myth that toads are poisonous carried over to the naming of toadstools, rounded cap-on-a-stalk fungi that are inedible or poisonous.

A toadstone is a gem or fossil tooth once believed to have formed in and survived the body of a toad, thus giving it magical or therapeutic powers.

Dr. Rebecca Pyles of the Herpetologists' League explains, "All amphibians have some poison glands in their skin ... one of the most poisonous is a tree frog, *Phyllobates terribilis*, one inch long, that has enough toxin to kill about 20,000 white mice or a couple of humans."

As for toads, there's usually no danger unless a person ingests one. Their warts don't exude poison and aren't warts, but bumps that aid in respiration and cooling. A big reason toads have a worse reputation than frogs in the West is the myth that kissing the right frog (presumably male) will turn it into a handsome prince! (Where frogs are moist and jump, toads are dry and walk on all fours.)

Toadflax is a slender-leaved plant with yellow or purplish flowers similar to snapdragons.

A toadfish resides in warm seas, has a wide head and big mouth and emits loud grunts!

Toady is also an Australian name for pufferfish, a wide-bodied fish that inflates itself, balloon-like, when it feels threatened.

Toad-in-the-hole, despite its name, is a delicious British dish of sausages baked in batter, usually served with brown sauce or gravy.

Drunk as a Newt

A newt is a small and slender amphibian that resembles some lizards. This expression derives from British gentlemen of the 17th and 18th centuries nicknaming certain small, slender boys newts. They looked after the men's horses while they spent the night gambling or drinking or in opium dens. The men would usually send out a "warm-up" drink to the newts, the better to keep them at their stations and treating the animals well. But the drinks were typically alcoholic and by the time the gents came out to retrieve their horses, the poor newts were often drunk.

Newt was originally ewt but with time and poor enunciation an ewt became a newt. Rather similar to the (deliberate) change of 1960s actress Carolyn Lee's name to Carol Lynley.

Lizards

A lounge lizard was traditionally a lounge musician. The derogatory term indicated he was tasteless and tacky—which image has largely transferred to the stereotypical Vegas lounge singer. As the phrase spread into non-musical general usage, it became affixed to well-dressed though perhaps crude young men (sometimes wearing lizard, alligator, or snakeskin shoes) who hung around venues where they could meet rich, usually older women. For example, afternoon tea dances such as the pre-stardom Rudolph Valentino frequented. The term alluded to the cool, calculating reptilian quality of a gigolo. Then and now, a lounge lizard was considered a social parasite; today he's most likely to be a nightclub habitué.

"Leapin' lizards!" was an alliterative catchphrase popularized by the comic-strip character Little Orphan Annie.

Best known as the stage and screen Auntie Mame, Rosalind Russell had a husband-manager, also a producer, who maneuvered to get her A-movie projects, for instance the film version of Ethel Merman's stage smash *Gypsy*. The gay or bisexual manager-producer, whom Russell met through his ex-boyfriend Cary Grant, was unpopular in Hollywood, where he was known as the Lizard of Roz.

Crocodile Tears

This phrase for insincere grief is one of the oldest on record, going back to ancient Egypt, where crocodiles proliferated in the Nile (hunting and human overpopulation have drastically reduced their numbers). After eating, crocodiles shed excess salt from glands beneath each eye, which makes it appear they're crying. Ancient Egyptians believed that after devouring its victim the crocodile was filled with remorse.

Sir Francis Bacon (1561–1626) wrote, "It is the wisdom of the crocodiles, that shed tears when they would devour." It was a long while until someone figured out that the "tears" had nil to do with sadness or guilt, as noted in the Victorian nursery rhyme "Natural History," which asks, "What are young men made of?" and answers, "Sighs and leers, and crocodile tears."

Crocodiles and alligators, viewed from a distance by exploring Europeans, were the basis of Western tales of dragons. Some observers "reported" that the reptiles' nostrils exuded clouds of smoke or even fire.

Gatorade was created in the mid 1960s at the University of Florida, home of the Gators, to replace fluids and salts lost during extreme exertion, like playing football. The drink's color is pale green, though most green alligators are found in cartoons and comic strips.

Did you know the tongues of crocodilians—crocs, gators, caimans, etc.—are fixed to the floor of their mouths? Now you do.

Snake Oil

Everyone's seen movies set in the Old West featuring itinerant snake-oil salesmen peddling phony medicines, nostrums, and elixirs. Did people truly believe they were buying snake oil and that it was good for you? In fact, the original snake oil came from Chinese water snakes and was used to treat almost any complaint. It may have arrived in the US via Chinese immigration following the 1849 gold rush. The oil was actually serpent fat, rather disgusting, but later found to be rich in omega-3 fatty acids; anti-inflammatory, it often helped ease arthritis and bursitis.

Once the product found a growing market, out from under the rocks crawled unscrupulous salesmen willing to state any claim and sell any fake product to make a buck. Such swindlers became so common that their sham goods became generically known as snake oil, that is to say, worthless. As for the real thing, it faded away, victim to changing tastes, anti-Chinese sentiment and laws, and newer medicines.

Snakes

To cherish or nurture a snake in one's bosom is to have one's kindness repaid with treachery. (Note Shakespeare's "how sharper than a serpent's tooth" re the ingratitude of some children.)

A snake in the grass is a hidden, treacherous enemy—a back-biter, as it were. (The phrase parallels a gorilla in the mist.)

Snakes and ladders is a well-known British children's game wherein one moves counters up ladders or down snakes illustrated on the board according to throws of a dice.

Snake eyes is a throw of two ones with a pair of dice.

A snake's head is a fritillary, a plant in the lily family with hanging bell-like flowers checkered in purple and red. A fritillary is also a butterfly with brown-orange wings checkered with black, the name from Latin for dice box.

A snakehead is a member of a Chinese criminal organization primarily involved in smuggling illegal immigrants to the West.

To "scotch the snake" is a British phrase for spoiling a plan. Snaky means angry or cranky in Australia and New Zealand.

A snakeboard is a trademarked skateboard of greater maneuverability and speed than the average board thanks to two footplates joined together by a bar.

Snakebite is a British drink comprising equal parts draught cider and lager, while snakebitten is a nearly obsolete North American term for unlucky.

A snakebird is also known as a darter and has a long neck and long pointy bill to spear fish with. Snake mackerel is another name for escolar, an elongated predatory fish with ringed markings around the eyes that resemble spectacles and in the 1800s gave it the name, which is Spanish for scholar.

Snakeroot is a North American plant supposed to yield an antidote to snake venom. It's also a plant with snakelike roots that produces medicinal drugs.

Snake-hipped describes someone with slim or minimal hips that moves in a sinuous way.

And a plumber's snake is a long flexible wire for removing obstacles from piping.

FYI: Do snakes sneeze? Very ssseldom. They expel fluid from their respiratory passages with a sudden blast of air from their lungs. As for flicking their forked tongues, it's not meant to intimidate nor is it preparatory to a bite. Rather, a snake's tongue helps detect prey and predators.

Dinosaur…

To call someone a dinosaur is less to imply that they're extremely old, more to declare they're hopelessly outdated, usually in their thinking, and haven't adapted to the modern era.

A dinosaur may also be a thing that's inefficient or so large it's unwieldy. Which hardly applies to those very efficient reptiles, large or small, who roamed the earth for far longer than humans have. It took an asteroid crashing into the earth from out of space about 65 million years ago to kill them off.

For many years, the Sinclair Oil Company used a dinosaur named (what else?) Dino as its mascot. It symbolized that petroleum comes from fossil fuels. The success of Dino was largely child-related. Children wanted to stop at the gas station with the dinosaur, and parents often indulged them.

As most every child knows, "dinosaur" is from ancient Greek words meaning terrible lizard. And of course Barney is a friendly six-foot purple dinosaur.

Worm

A startling fact: worms comprise some three-quarters of all animal life on the planet. Obviously, worms are crucial to life on—and under—earth, but their lowly state and primitive form have rendered them verbally defamed. Calling somebody a worm means they're low and contemptible. Or weak, though how weak are worms when they're 75 percent of life on earth?

Computer-wise, a worm is a detrimentally self-replicating program. To worm one's way in is to sneak or crawl in, usually with ill intention; to worm something out of someone is to do so by underhanded means.

Metaphorically, a worm's eye view is the lowest or humblest possible vantage point.

Shakespeare wrote, "The worm has turned," indicating a reversal of fortune. The phrase generally refers to a turnabout situation favoring the less powerful party, such as an employee versus an employer. It can also mean somebody meek or weak has become bold or strong.

To open a can of worms is to commence or pursue a subject that proves worse or more distasteful than one presumed.

Worm is a part of the names of several machine components, for instance, a wormwheel is the wheel of a worm gear. Worm gears are driven by a steam engine. Worm is also used to describe some worm-shaped items (like gummy worms) and creatures, usually parasitic.

A worm cast is a twistingly coiled mass of mud, soil, or sand thrown up to the surface by a burrowing worm.

Nautically, to worm is to smooth a rope by winding thread between its strands.

In physics, a wormhole is a hypothetical connection between vastly separated areas of space-time.

A worm lizard is a reptile which, like a worm, is subterranean, burrows, is blind, segmented, and limbless. Interestingly, in many fairy tales worm is interchangeable with dragon—that is, a *big* worm (think *Dune*).

Woodworm, Wormwood...

A woodworm isn't a worm—it's the wood-boring larva of a furniture beetle. Woodworm is also the negative condition of wood damaged by this larva. Worm-eaten also describes the holes made by this non-worm. Likewise, a bookworm—not the well-read human type—is the larva of another wood-boring beetle that feeds off the paper and glue in books.

Wormwood also has nothing to do with worms. It's a bitter-tasting shrub used in the making of vermouth, absinthe, and certain medicines. (Vermouth's name is from the German

Vermut, or wormwood.) Wormseed is a plant whose seeds can be used in treating parasitic-worm infestations.

Ringworm isn't a worm, but an itchy, contagious skin disease of the scalp or feet caused by fungi. A hookworm is an actual worm, a parasite that latches onto the wall of the intestines using hooklike mouthparts.

Nor is a shipworm a worm, but a mollusk related to clams that leaves telltale holes made through hard cellulose fibers.

Vermin

Vermicelli is a fine pasta. In Italian it means little worms. In Britain, vermicelli are chocolate shreds used for decorating cakes.

The Latin for worm is *vermis*, for little worm *vermiculus*. From the former derives our word vermin. From the latter, the red shade vermilion, via a small Mediterranean insect which when crushed yields a brilliant red dye. The insect's modern name, kermes, originated the red-shade names crimson and carmine.

Vermicular means worm-shaped or relating to intestinal worms. Vermiculated signifies worm-eaten or marked with undulating lines.

Vermiculite is an unusual brown or yellow mineral sometimes used for thermal insulation that, when it expands because of heat, emits shapes resembling small worms!

Vermifuge is a medicine that gets rid of parasitic worms and of course vermicide is a substance that kills worms.

(Which recalls the old rhyme: By the sewer he lived, by the sewer he died; they said it was murder, but it was sewer-cide.)

Spiders

"'Come into my parlor,' said the spider to the fly." Neither insects nor "bugs," spiders are arachnids—the family includes scorpions and ticks—with eight legs and eight eyes that spin webs to capture insect prey. They help keep the vermin population down yet have an unsavory reputation. A few reasons: they're considered awfully hairy (especially close-up), are thought poisonous (most aren't), and the fear of the female black widow spider (deadlier than the male). At least their webs are beautiful.

A spider is also a long-legged rest for a billiard cue that may be positioned above a ball without touching it.

In Britain, a spider keeps a load in place on a vehicle via a set of radiating elastic ties.

Computerwise, spider is another name for crawler, a program that scans the Internet so it can create an index of data.

A spider mite is a tiny plant-feeding mite said, via magnification, to resemble a small spider.

A spider monkey is a South American monkey with an especially long tail and limbs.

A spider plant is a member of the lily family with long, thin leaves striped yellow and native to South Africa.

Spiderwort is an American plant whose flowers have long hairy stamens—the fertilizing male organs of flowers. (Wort, which haplessly sounds like wart, simply indicates a plant or herb formerly used as food or medicine, e.g., butterwort.)

The Spider King was the sobriquet of 15th-century monarch Louis XI, whose web of plots and spies enmeshed France. His paranoia was partly fed by the cowardly and corrupt legacy of his father Charles VII, whom Joan of Arc had virtually made king before he allowed her to be burned at the stake.

Two spidery expressions are "to blow the cobwebs away," meaning to void one's mind of old-fashioned ideas, and "to be at the center of the spider's web"—to control a complex group or operation.

FYI, the biggest spider is the female Goliath Tarantula of South America, whose leg span is ten inches, the size of a dinner plate. The smallest spider is the male Patu Digua, whose body is smaller than a pinhead.

Cobweb

Back when it was thought all spiders were poisonous they were called, in Olde English, attercoppes, meaning poison head. So the spun creation of a spider was a copweb. With time and imprecise pronunciation, it became cobweb.

Spider comes from Olde English spinnan, to draw out and twist fiber, also the source of spin (spider in German is *Spinne*). The word is used in names of other creatures usually distinguished by long, thin legs, like the sea spider and spider crab.

Spiders' worst enemies are other spiders. Yes, they're cannibals and can get caught in each other's webs. Pirate spiders prey exclusively on fellow spiders.

Tarantism

Talk about a dancing fool. Tarantism is a psychological malady consisting of an extreme impulse to dance. This condition, most prevalent in southern Italy from the 15th to 17th centuries, was thought to be caused by the bite of a tarantula, an impressively large, hairy spider sometimes known as the wolf spider in southern Europe and also found in the subtropical Americas. It was named after the Italian seaport of Taranto, which also gave its name to tarantism.

A possible cure for the above was the southern Italian dance called the Tarantella—after the tarantula, which was wrongly believed poisonous (most are not). Gina Lollobrigida, who performed the dance with a beribboned tambourine in a memorable episode of the 1980s nighttime TV soap *Falcon Crest*, explained, "It is a fast dance. You whirl and spin … it is graceful but very fast and tiring, and if you do it correctly, it will remove all the poisons from inside you. It leaves you healthy and strong."

Conversely, many people at the benighted time believed the Tarantella was the result of the terpsichorean illness, that it was the one dance the afflicted couldn't help breaking into.

Vinegaroons, found in Texas and the American South, are similar to tarantulas but smell like vinegar when they're crushed.

A once-popular nickname for whiskey was tarantula juice. Bottoms down!

Bugs

The word bug, which covers a host of tiny creatures, is of unknown origin.

How cute is a bug in a rug? Sometimes the media—or in the past, famous columnists—like to reverse meanings or substitute words. In the 1940s the phrase was "snug as a bug in a rug." Somebody substituted cute for snug, and it took.

"Cute as a June bug" flatters the chafer, a large beetle that often flies in June.

Having or getting a bug may denote enthusiasm, for example, "She's caught the acting bug."

A bug can be a hidden microphone, as when spies or government agencies bug a telephone. A bug is also a microorganism that's caused an illness, as in "I must have caught a bug." A bug may be an error in a computer program or system, and bug off (sometimes buzz off) means go away!

Bugbane is a tall plant with fernlike leaves once used to eliminate bedbugs. (Bane comes from *bana*, a Germanic word for poison.)

Various words with bug in them, like bugger, baby buggy, etc., have naught to do with insects.

When commercials feature bugs or insects as themselves, the public usually reacts adversely. But when bugs have been given individual, human-seeming—albeit nasty—personalities, as in ads for Bardahl automotive products or Raid insecticide, they've helped boost sales. In the 1950s when the US government started its anti-litter campaign, their mascot was the litterbug, a roguish-looking creature wearing an eye patch, with a cigarette dangling out the side of his mouth.

Cricket

The British game wasn't named after the insect related to the grasshopper but with shorter legs. The expression it's not cricket, meaning not fair, is from the game, which existed by the 1300s. Among the first to use the expression were the townsmen of Boxgrove, England, who in 1622 were prosecuted for playing the game on a Sunday.

The insect's onomatopoeic name comes from Old French *criquer*, to crackle, supposedly imitative of the musical chirping sound a male cricket makes. To be as merry or chirpy or lively as a cricket reflects human perception of what has been called the happiest insect. Jiminy Cricket all but stole the animated feature *Pinocchio* from its eponymous protagonist and had his own hit song, "When You Wish Upon a Star."

Jiminy Cricket is a minced oath, that is, an exclamation in which one or more words have substituted for a word that's taboo or considered sacred. Thus, "Jiminy Cricket!" in place of Jesus Christ!

The expression to be knee-high to a grasshopper—or a duck—means since somebody was a small child or as tall as a small child.

If you've wondered whether male crickets' legs get sore or chapped from rubbing together so much, they don't. Their legs are made of hardy material similar to our fingernails. The chaps' legs can wear down eventually, but do grow back.

Crazy Bugs

Bughouse derives from a flea-infested hotel that could drive a person crazy. By the 1940s the term was being used in novels to mean a psychiatric hospital or lunatic asylum or somebody who was crazy, often under the influence of drugs.

Buggy also came to mean nuts or very disturbed. Besides alliteration, that wascally Warner Bros. wabbit was named Bugs Bunny partly because he was goofy and sometimes went off his rocker. Alliteration applies to many cartoon characters' names, regardless of the language. For instance in Spanish Donald Duck is el Pato Pascual, *pato* meaning duck.

A bugaboo is related to a bugbear, something that causes great fear or is used to scare children, from the obsolete word bogey or bug, possibly of Celtic origin and referring to the devil.

To have the jitters is to be nervous or move irregularly. Parents in the 1940s were often nervous about the movements involved in the jitterbug, a fast dance performed to swing music that took young America by storm.

A fire-bug is someone who compulsively watches or sets fires. The use of bug in this term expresses mental obsession.

To bug someone—non-mechanically—is to be irksome, a pest, driving them to distraction.

(Ask your friends which animal causes more human deaths every year than any other? They'll usually guess snakes, sharks, lions, tigers, mad dogs, etc., none of which come close to: the mosquito.)

Canapés

Contrary to the Three Stooges' Curly, canapés are not a can of peas, but elegant appetizers, usually served on a cracker or melba toast. In French, *canapé* means sofa. What's that got to do with animals?

The Greek word for mosquito was *konops*. A *konopeion* was a primitive mosquito net—curtains hung around a sofa or a piece of furniture to recline on.

In Latin this was adapted to *conopeum*, in medieval Latin to *canopeum*, in Middle English to canope, then finally our canopy (which is atop rather than around a bed, not sofa). The French used *canapé* to describe the sofa, not the curtains. And where do guests usually eat a canapé? On a sofa—or chair.

Since only female mosquitoes eat blood, what do male mosquitoes live on? Nectar, which is what all mosquitoes eat most of the time. Only a female has the biting mouth-part to pierce human or animal skin. The amount of blood she draws is scarcely missed by a human but may be greater than her body weight. The lipids in blood are converted into protein and iron that increase her fecundity. After a meal of nectar, she can lay five or ten eggs; after blood, 200.

Pests...

A pest is a destructive insect or any other animal that harms human food, crops, or livestock. Also an annoying person who pesters you. Its origin is the Latin *pestis*, plague (in French, one of Albert Camus's best-known novels is *La Peste*, The Plague).

A pest-house used to be a hospital for people with infectious diseases, particularly the plague. Pestiferous means harboring infection and disease. Pestilence is a fatal epidemic, especially bubonic plague. And a pesticide is something that hopefully offs pests.

A tick is a very small parasitic arachnid that latches onto skin in order to draw blood. The expression full as a tick refers to it becoming bloated with blood, much heavier than before its meal. In Britain a tick is a worthless or disreputable person—often a parasite.

A nit is the egg or young of a louse, and in Britain a stupid person. The 1961 novel *Marnie* (from which Hitchcock made a memorable movie) used the then-common expression as nervous as a nit about its larcenous—but far from stupid—protagonist. To nit-pick is to fault-find about details as tiny as a nit.

A rare non-negative insect phrase is "to put out feelers"— to try and gauge others' opinions or feelings before making a decision.

Lice

Lice is the plural of louse. There are many kinds, but basically a louse is a small parasitic insect. When a louse is a lousy or contemptible person, the plural is louses, as when Marilyn Monroe sings "It's then that those louses go back to their spouses" in the song "Diamonds Are a Girl's Best Friend." Oddly, in German a male may affectionately call his girl-friend *meine kleine Lausbube*, my little louse baby.

Lice can't fly or jump, so with their six legs they cling to human hair and suck blood, biting through the scalp. The amount is miniscule, but the lice then lay eggs that hatch in eight to ten days, then become adults in a week to ten days— a louse lives about a month. Besides head lice, which occur most often in children, there are pubic lice, usually sexually transmitted and also known as crabs, and body lice from poor hygiene, often called cooties, a word that originated during the First World War, possibly from the Malay *kutu*, a parasitic biting insect.

Soldiers helped popularize the negative adjective lousy (which came from infested with lice), also to be lousy with something, that is, to have a lot of it—e.g., "She's lousy with sex appeal"—plus louse meaning somebody unliked. After WWII all three terms became popular with American teenagers, then the first and third worked their way into general usage, especially the first.

A louse fly (rhymes with house fly) is a flattened blood-sucking fly that spends much or most of its life on a single host.

Lousewort is an herbaceous plant that's partly parasitic and was formerly thought to harbor lice.

A Fly in the Ointment

Many centuries ago it was believed a single fly in the ointment spoiled the medicinal whole and robbed it of its efficacy. The Bible's Ecclesiastes (10:1) says, "Dead flies cause the ointment of the apothecary to send forth a stinking savour." Discovering a fly, living or dead, was more serious then because remedies hardly ever came in individual portions, but in huge vats that could treat a hundred or more people.

A Flea in One's Ear

John Lyly was a popular Elizabethan writer who in 1579 published *Euphues, or the Anatomy of Wit*. It included a vignette in which an aristocrat chastises a servant: "Ferardo ... whispering Philautus in his eare (who stoode as though he had a flea in his eare), desired him to keepe silence." The analogy was a dog with an actual flea in its ear, shaking its head in annoyance.

Another analogy was fleas trapped in the armor of ancient knights. Discomfort was again implied, but the eventual meaning was to tell somebody off. (Georges Feydeau's raucous 1907 French farce is titled *A Flea in Her Ear*.)

Flea Circus

Piqued by the jumping prowess of fleas, people have trained them for millennia. A flea can jump up to 12 inches, 150 times its length; for a human, that's equivalent to jumping over 800 feet. Flea circuses began in England in the 1600s and peaked in popularity during the 1830s when Signo Bertolotto toured Europe with his performing fleas that danced, pulled coaches, and actually wore costumes. Swiss watchmakers created teeny circus vehicles for the fleas.

But it wasn't all merriment, for the fleas were permanently glued to each other or to the miniscule chains with which they pulled wagons (fleas can pull 160,000 times their own weight, comparable to a human pulling 12,000 tons).

In time, flea circuses became popular at county fairs throughout the US. Though rare, they still exist, the creatures no longer glued to one another or to props. One way of training fleas is with tuning forks, using frequencies pleasant and unpleasant to fleas. Most flea circuses used human fleas; most have been replaced with cat fleas. In recent years San Francisco, Winston-Salem (NC), and Providence (RI) have boasted popular flea circuses.

Dogs are unwelcome at performances because flea owners fear losing their star attractions.

Fleas

Fleas are wingless jumping insects that live on the blood of birds and mammals, including cats and dogs, thus the flea collar. Few species bother humans, though over 250 kinds are found in North America. "Flea" is of Germanic origin.

Flea markets originated in Paris, where the translated name meant just that. Since the goods were secondhand and bargain-rate, it was assumed some of them would include fleas. Truth in advertising—what a concept.

Fleapit often referred to a pre-cineplex theatre or cinema that was seedy and not in its hygienic prime.

A fleabag is most likely a run-down, dingy hotel or other dump.

Fleabitten is either literal or something or someone that's dilapidated or infested with disreputability.

A flea beetle is a small jumping leaf beetle that may target members of the cabbage family.

Fleabane and fleawort, members of the daisy family (sweet!), are plants reputed to drive off fleas.

Flea glass was the pre-microscope name of the magnifying instrument which Dutch scientist Anton Van Leeuwenhoek, "the father of microbiology," helped develop so he could study fleas.

The saying fit as a flea implies excellent health, alluding to a flea's strength and its being full of life-nourishing blood (so's a vampire).

Dragonfly

It's not a dragon (nothing is) and not a fly, but partly because its body is longer than most insects' and it's aggressively predatory, in English it's called a dragonfly. Perhaps the first time it was called that was in 1626 in Francis Bacon's *Sylva Sylvarum: or a Natural Historie in Ten Centuries*. Previously, it was variously known as an Adder Bolt, a Snake Doctor—it was actually believed dragonflies could bring snakes back to life—a Horse Stinger, Devil's Riding Horse, and Devil's Darning Needle, from the belief that if one fell asleep by a stream (where dragonflies are often found) the insect might sew your eyes shut.

A possible if specialized explanation for the name is that in Romanian it translated to Devil's Fly and in Romanian devil and dragon are *dracul* (the diminutive is *dracula*). In medieval times and earlier, the "devil" was often represented as a dragon, as in the St. George-and-the-dragon story.

There are over 5,000 species of dragonflies in the world. They live six months to seven years—a long time for an insect—have large eyes with some 30,000 lenses, sport two pairs of wings that allow them to not flap so hard or often, and they eat mosquitoes, ants, bees, and wasps. In turn, they're eaten by birds, lizards, frogs, fish, spiders, and ... bigger dragonflies. They're usually near water because their voracious larvae are aquatic.

Dragon...

In the West, snakes and dragons symbolize evil. In the East, not so—look at snakes in India and dragons in Chinese mythology (China's zodiac includes the Year of the Dragon). In the West, when a person is called a dragon, it's a female, defined by the *Concise Oxford English Dictionary* as "derogatory—a fierce and intimidating woman." Dragon lady was similarly applied to certain East Asian women.

To chase the dragon is a euphemism for smoking heroin.

A bearded dragon is a semi-arboreal Australian lizard with spiny scales and a big throat pouch featuring sharp spines.

A dragonfish is a long, slim deep-sea fish with a fleshy filament growing from its chin, fang-like teeth, and luminous organs! A dragonet is a small fish the male of which bears bright colors.

A dragon tree is native to the Canary Islands (remember them?), is palmlike, grows slowly, and yields dragon's blood, a red gum or powder produced by the tree's stem.

Dragon boats feature a traditional Chinese design resembling a dragon and are paddle-propelled. A dragon ship is the traditional Viking longship decorated with a beaked prow.

Snapdragons are plants with brightly colored two-lobed flowers that supposedly gape like a hungry dragon's mouth when a bee lands on the curved lip.

A dragoon is a member of various British cavalry regiments, historically a mounted infantryman armed with a carbine which, like a dragon, was supposed to breathe fire. To dragoon is to coerce someone into doing something.

A dragonnade was a form of oppression by a conquering power that imposed the inconvenient and costly quartering of its troops on a population.

Buffalo Bee

One of the 1950s' most popular commercial animal mascots was Nabisco's Buffalo Bee, modeled on Buffalo Bill but voiced by Mae Questl, who'd done the voices of Betty Boop and Olive Oyl (Popeye's skinny girlfriend). She later offered, "A bee is such a perfect ad symbol. They work hard, they're small and fuzzy, kids love them, and they make honey! All you have to worry about is the sting." The cute critter, who had no stinger—two six-shooters, instead—wore a cowboy hat, striped shirt, and red bandanna. Besides advertising Wheat Honeys and Rice Honeys cereals, Buffalo Bee starred in his own comic books. However, by the early '60s western shows and themes were waning in popularity, and Buffalo Bee was one of the casualties.

Most of the buzzing one hears from a bee is the vibrations of its wings during flight—flapping over 200 times per second. And though bees and hives seem synonymous, about 90 percent of bees are solitary, unlike the social bees: honeybees, bumblebees, and stingless bees.

Bees

"The bee's knees" is another example of the importance of alliteration and assonance in coining popular phrases. In the 1700s there was "big as a bee's knee." In the 1800s there was "weak as a bee's knee." The 1920s produced "the bee's knees," which meant terrific—as did that decade's "the cat's meow," its whiskers, and pajamas.

A bee-line was born of the apian habit of social bees flying back to their hive in a straight line. Busy as a bee is self-explanatory, but the stereotype doesn't fit all bees.

To have a bee in one's bonnet is to be upset or obsessed with something.

To drone on about something is to talk monotonously and seemingly endlessly, probably related to a bee's long low humming sound. A drone is a male bee that doesn't work but can fertilize the queen bee. A drone is also an unpiloted, remote-controlled aircraft.

A human queen bee is a woman who's reached the top and wants no female competition or camaraderie—like late Prime Minister Margaret Thatcher. A 1955 movie by that title aptly starred Joan Crawford.

Mad as a hornet comes from the angry-seeming stings of that insect, which is a large wasp. Waspish is excessively irritable or sharp.

The obsolete wasp-waist on a severely corseted woman derives from the narrow waist of a wasp.

It's been said that a WASP (White Anglo-Saxon Protestant) is so initialed because the powerful American group has often used its waspish tongue and metaphorical sting on assorted minority groups. Spelling and quilting bees, though they may involve a swarm of people, are not of apian derivation.

Butterfly

Many theories have been put forward about why this beautiful creature is called a butterfly. Its name is also beautiful in Spanish—*mariposa*—in French—*papillon*—less so in German—*Schmetterling*. Samuel Johnson believed the insect was so named because butterflies show up in spring, when butter is churned. Another explanation is that butterflies' tiny dung is yellow (how could they tell?). More pertinent are the facts that England's most common butterfly, the brimstone, is butter-colored, and that a widespread myth during the Middle Ages held that fairies would fly and steal butter at night while in the shape of ... butterflies.

"Elusive as a butterfly" is self-explanatory. A butterfly mind is unable to concentrate for long on one subject, flitting from here to there.

A social butterfly is usually a frivolous or insincere woman trying to make an impression in society by going from one home to one party to one function to one gala to the next. The phrase may have originated in the 1860s, during the Victorian era, when crashing high society was often attempted but rarely successful.

Butterflies in one's stomach produce a fluttering sensation and denote stage fright or anxiety, but like real butterflies, they don't often stay too long.

To break a butterfly on a wheel means to employ excessive effort or force in achieving a result.

"Poor Butterfly" is a beautiful 1916 song about a pining female who waits, not flits (perhaps she should).

Then there's the butterfly stroke in swimming and the butterfly nut—another name for a wing nut—also the butterfly valve, not to mention (too late now) the theoretical butterfly effect from the 1980s referring to chaos theory and local change yielding larger change elsewhere, as with a butterfly fluttering in Rio de Janeiro possibly changing the weather in Chicago.

Moths

Moths are the more drably colored, less glamorous cousins of butterflies. Differences include their wings resting flat instead of erect, the lack of clubbed antennae, and not being active by day.

Moths are drawn to light, thus the expression "like a moth to a flame" describing particular human attractions.

Moth-eaten may be literal or can be old-fashioned, like moth-eaten ideas.

As for mothballs, which male moths don't have, they're often made of naphthalene and deter clothes moths. In mothballs signifies in storage or on hold. And unless you're a lepidopterist, that's about all that can be said about moths.

Except that moths and butterflies have no noses and breathe through spiracles—holes in the sides of their bodies. Spiracles include teensy-weensy valves that keep out water and dust. There.